A PILGRIM'S GUIDE TO

Sarria - Santiago

The last 7 stages of the
Camino de Santiago *Francés*
O Cebreiro - Sarria - Santiago

T0054475

*A Practical & Mystical Manual
for the Modern-day Pilgrim*

John Brierley

ISBN: 978-1-122216-35-2

British Library Cataloguing-in-Publication Data.
A catalogue record for this book is available from the British Library.

Printed and bound in Czechia

CAMINO GUIDES
An imprint of Kaminn Media Ltd
272 Bath Street,
Glasgow, G2 4JR

Tel: +44 (0)141 354 1758
Fax: +44 (0)141 354 1759

Email: info@caminoguides.com
www.caminoguides.com

7 STAGE SUMMARY – ROUTE MAPS & TOWN GUIDES

Welcome to The Way of St. James *el camino de Sant Iago*. And specifically to the final stages of the French Way *camino francés* through Galicia. Unlike many other pilgrim routes to Santiago de Compostela, the waymarking on the *camino francés* is now very extensive. The familiar yellow arrow *flecha amarilla* will become a source of great comfort to you along the way – popping into view just when you think you are lost. This said, an accurate map and guidebook is useful to help you plan your itinerary and excursions and to put you back on the path when your mind wanders and your feet follow!

A pilgrimage takes place upon two paths - the *outer* path on which our feet tread and the *inner* path of soul. In the following pages I have endeavoured to find a balance between the two by paying equal respect to both. That is why these guides are subtitled *a practical **and** mystical manual for the modern-day pilgrim*. That we might find a place to lay our weary head at the end of the day but also, and crucially, that we might feel supported and encouraged to dive into the mysteries of our individual soul awakenings.

Pilgrimage offers us an opportunity to slow down and allow some spaciousness into our lives. It encourages us to ask the perennial question – Who am I? And, crucially, it provides time for answers to be understood. We may find that Santiago is not the end of the way but the beginning of something entirely new. Whichever route we take, our ultimate destination is assured. The only choice we have is how long it takes us to arrive. *Buen camino – John.*

ABOUT THE AUTHOR: *John Brierley 1948–2023.* For a quarter of a century the Caminos de Santiago inspired John Brierley. He fervently believed in their inherent power to foster positive change, in our individual lives and in the world through changing the way we view our place in it. These guides are the product of a calling he felt to

John in Santaigo. Portrait by Patti Silva

encourage pilgrims to embark on both an *outer* journey, as well as to consider their steps along an *inner* journey. The following pages are filled with his enthusiasm and profound belief in the importance of both. They also contain clear and concise information on where to find a cup of coffee in the morning, a ritual as important to him as prayer.

In 2023 John took his final steps on this earthly pilgrimage, but his passion, wisdom and energy live on in the works he left behind. While the practical information in these guides continues to be updated by his daughter, the message is, and will always remain his. To make each step a prayer, to open our hearts with loving kindness and always to keep exploring - both the *outer* world around us and our own *inner* landscape.

NOTES TO THIS EDITION: This guide features the final stages of the Camino Francés through Galicia. It was created in response to requests from the numerous pilgrims who walk only the final stretch of this ancient route, so they need not carry the weight of unnecessary information. While we are delighted to grant a request that serves pilgrims the necessity of this guides creation is thought provoking. In 2003, when the first edition of our guide to the Camino Francés was published, the total number of pilgrims recorded on this route was 65,453. Of these 16% (10,333) began their journey in Sarria, 117 km from Santiago. The second two most popular staring points, St Jean Pied de Port and Roncesvalles, each attracted a 12% share of pilgrims and both are over 750 km from Santiago. In 2023 total pilgrims on the Camino Francés have risen to over 219,000 but notably the percentage of those commencing their journey is Sarria has leapt from 16% to 61%. This raises an obvious question with a less obvious answer... why are so many more people seeking a shorter pilgrimage today compared to 20 years ago?

The optimist in me celebrates the increasing popularity and accessibility of pilgrimage, regardless of length, as every journey is valid and important. The pessimist in me questions the pressures that modern life is placing on us and the role that may play in this trend. Within the context of increasing financial burdens and rising cost of living, the squeezing of earnings and holidays - "time out" is an increasingly hard won prize. Yet in these circumstances I would argue that the space provided by pilgrimage is needed more than ever.

The reasons people choose to walk this section of the camino are numerous. Some of us would love to have the time to begin our journey on the French side of the Pyrenees, the starting point which gives this route its name, but are prevented by practicalities. Others will have no desire or need to spend more than a week on the path. Some will be seeking to ensure they walk the last 100 km into Santiago required to receive a *compostela* (the official certificate of completion). Others may not realise that there are options to walk other routes or from further afield. Whatever *your* reason, we wish you well on your way. However, if external pressures have influenced your choice of a shorter pilgrimage we invite you to consider how you might maximise the impact of your experience. What is it you hope you gain from your time immersed on the camino and is there anything you can do to ensure that you achieve or receive it? Time is no indicator of depth but with less time we may need to be more conscious of how we use it.

We continue to inhabit a world where change seems to be the only constant. We trust that, despite the inevitability of change, the information here will be more than ample to guide you gracefully to Santiago. Along the way you will meet fellow wanderers and the locals whose land you pass through. But above all you may meet your Self, and that may make all the difference.

Journey well. *Buen Camino.*

Before you go: This section has more detailed notes on preparation.

WHEN TO GO?

SPRING: If you like peace and quiet, the months of March and April will provide fewer other pilgrims and tourists. Hostels will be opening and flights and ferries should be operating, at least on a limited basis. You will be accompanied by early spring flowers and cool conditions for walking, although the nights are likely to be cold and rain plentiful, especially in the mountain areas of Galicia. Pack additional wet gear and warm fleeces. May/June will be warmer but also busier.

SUMMER: These months can be very hot and accommodation in short supply. July & August can be particularly busy and if this coincides with a Holy Year (any year when St. James Day, 25th July, falls on a Sunday) it can be difficult for those wanting a quiet and introspective experience. These 2 months alone account for almost half of all pilgrims arriving in Santiago for the whole year. September is also becoming busy.

AUTUMN: Late September through October often provides more stable weather than spring, the fierce heat of summer is over, the snow hasn't yet arrived and most hostels are still open. Because of this, the period is becoming more popular but it will still be quieter than the summer months.

WINTER: If you are an experienced walker the winter can provide some of the most mystical experiences and you'll have much of the camino to yourself. Though many hostels close between the end of October and March (Easter) some remain open year round. Check the online and see *www.aprinca.com/alberguesinvierno* for a list of hostels that stay open all year. Bring warm waterproof clothes and remember that daylight hours are restricted, so the daily distance that you can walk is reduced.

WEATHER: The weather in northern Spain, particularly Galicia, is very unpredictable. The **summer** months may see temperatures soar to over 35 Celsius (95 Fahrenheit) and the nights are often uncomfortably warm. Sun protection is essential including a hat *sombrero*. Carry plenty of water to replace fluids lost through physical exertion and the heat.

In **winter** the higher ground can be blocked with snow with temperatures dropping below freezing. In the shoulder seasons, you can expect anything in between. Be prepared for any eventuality. **Daylight hours** can be important when planning each day's stage. In the summer you have all the hours God made and certainly more than you could walk! In mid winter, your daylight is reduced to 8 hours maximum.

Keep in mind the interim accommodation listed in this guide and adjust daily stages when needed. In the winter when daylight is at a premium and you want to be settled in your accommodation before dusk you may wish to shorten the length you walk in a day. But be aware of the limited lodging in the winter months. Likewise in the height of summer when the midday heat can be exhausting to walk through. In this case you may wish to set off early and aim to be finished walking by lunchtime, or take a lengthy break in the heat of the day before continuing on in the afternoon. Be flexible and find a rhythm that suits you and your needs.

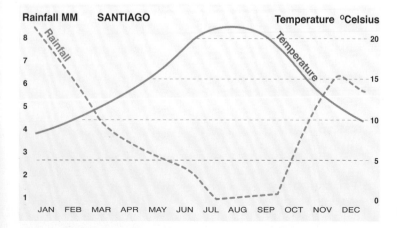

Rainfall MM   SANTIAGO   Temperature °Celsius

Rainfall / Temperature chart for Santiago, months JAN–DEC. Left axis Rainfall MM 1–8, right axis Temperature °Celsius 0–20.

Some Statistics: While we can never know the actual number of pilgrims who arrive into Santiago each year, we do know from records kept at the Pilgrim Office *www.oficinadelperegrino.com* that over 444,000 pilgrims collected a Compostela in 2023. The ever increasing popularity of the caminos, it seems, knows no bounds.

50% of people arrived via the Camino Francés, making it by far the most populous route, with Sarria being the busiest starting point.

40% of pilgrims gave a religious reason for their journey while 48% gave a spiritual or 'other' reason for doing so. 93% arrived on foot, 5% by bicycle, 601 on horseback, 273 by boat and 194 by wheelchair.

197 nations were represented last year, the majority from: ❶ Spain: 196,734 (45%) ❷ USA 32,000 (7.3%) ❸ Italy 28,579 (6.5%) ❹ Germany 24,303 (5.5%) ❺ Portugal 20,594 (4.6%) ❻ France 10,571 (2.1%) ❼ UK 10,495 (2.4%) ❽ Mexico 8,245 (1.9%) ❾ Korea 7,482 (1.7%) ❿ Ireland 6,942 (1.6%) ⓫ Australia 6,797 (1.55%) ⓬ Canada 6,722 (1.5%).

Pilgrim numbers by year:

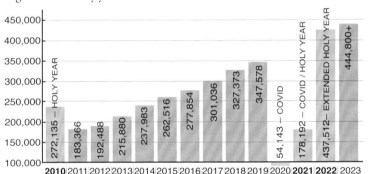

Pilgrim numbers by month:

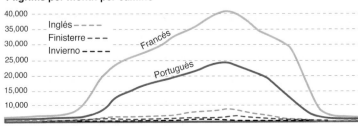

HOW TO GET THERE – *AND BACK*: (See **map** on inside back cover for airports and ferry terminals). *Note that schedules and prices are liable to change and reduced services can be expected during the winter months.* **Spanish Prefix: (+34)**

● **Arriving in O Cebreiro:** A new direct bus link between Santiago and O Cebreiro was inaugurated in 2021 making it easy to reach this significant starting point. Monbus run a daily service from €14 with a journey time of 3 hours. See *www.monbus.es* for schedule and bookings.

● **Arriving in Sarria:** The majority of pilgrims arrive in Sarria by bus from Santiago. Options include: ① Monbus *www.monbus.es* who operate a daily service direct from Santiago to Sarria, journey time approx 2 hours and €11. This bus also stops at Santiago airport (SCQ). ② Other options via bus are available with Alsa *www.alsa.es* and Freire - note these services are not direct and require a change at Lugo but may be useful if you require alternative departure times. ③ By train (with a change at Ourense) average journey time 4 hours, tickets €16 see RENFE *www.renfe.com/es*

❖ **Pilgrim Facilities: Pilgrim passport** *credencial* available at the Pilgrim office in Santiago or Iglesia de Santa Mariña on rúa Maior in Sarria. Pilgrims who require assistance can arrange for **backpack transfers** *transporte de mochilas* between reserved private accommodation (it is not possible to reserve in Xunta hostels). Contact: ●Pilbeo *www.pilbeo.com/en* ☎ 670 64 80 78 / ●Xacotrans: *www.xacotrans.com* ☎ (+34) 82 639 300 / ●El Camino con Correos *www.elcaminoconcorreos.com/en* The Spanish postal service *Correos* which also offers luggage storage in Santiago.

● **Arriving / Departing Santiago:** Travel costs vary widely but several budget airlines now compete for the traffic into Santiago - Rosalía de Castro international airport (SCQ) in Lavacolla. *Empresa Freire* offers a regular bus service from/to the city centre.

AIR: *Direct flights to Santiago:* ●*Easyjet* from London Gatwick, Geneva & Basle. ●*Ryanair* from London Stansted, Frankfurt & Milan. ●*Vueling* from London, Paris, Brussels, Amsterdam & Zurich. ●*Aer Lingus* from Dublin (summer schedule). ●*BA / Iberia* and other major airlines offer regular services throughout the year via various connecting airports in Spain, mainly Madrid. ●*Vueling* also fly direct from London to *A Coruña* and *Asturias*. Check other possibilities from / to nearby airports at A Coruña, Vigo and Porto – all of which have regular rail and bus connections to/from Santiago. Note schedules may change and be reduced during off peak season.

Rail: With obvious environmental benefits and due to uncertainties in the airline industry rail is likely to become more popular. You can book online through Spanish rail network RENFE *www.renfe.es/horarios/english* or Rail Europe at *www.raileurope.co.uk*.

Bus: you can book online with Alsa _www.alsa.es_ (paypal). Also check _www. monbus.es_ (both with english language option).

Ferry: The advantage of sailing is that you get a chance to acclimatise slowly. Check Brittany Ferries (Santander - Portsmouth).

Car Hire: a relatively cheap option (if sharing the cost) to travel to/from ports and airports. This option is only practicable within Spain as drop-off in another country (i.e Portugal) is prohibitively expensive.

TRAVEL NOTES:

_____
_____
_____
_____
_____
_____
_____
_____
_____
_____
_____
_____
_____
_____
_____
_____

ENVIRONMENTAL IMPACT OF TRAVEL
I am often asked why I endorse 'cheap' air travel to and from Santiago when it is so costly for the environment. I believe that walking the caminos can be a powerful catalyst for positive change so that the means (of getting there) justifies the end (expanded awareness). A central tenet of these guides is that pilgrimage starts the moment we become conscious that life itself is a sacred journey, carrying with it the responsibility to act accordingly.

All travel has an impact on the environment; none more so than air travel. We can, however, minimise the damaging emissions of greenhouse gases by choosing the most responsible mode of travel available to us and offsetting the amount produced in what is effectively a carbon sink. _www.seat61.com/ CO2flights.htm_ compares rail versus plane. _www.myclimate.org_ will calculate the amount of emissions produced from your departure point and what you would need to contribute to offset this. A return flight London to Santiago will produce 0.33 tonnes of CO_2 (rail reduces this by around 90%!) and the stakes go up if you're travelling from further afield. Carbon offsets don't solve the problem but can help orientate us towards finding solutions. The key aspect here is about raising awareness – not about producing guilt trips.

Pilgrim Passport *credencial:*
In order to stay at many pilgrim hostels and to receive the certificate of completion *compostela* you need to provide proof that you have walked at least the last 100 km into Santiago. This is done by having a pilgrim passport *credencial* stamped (*sello*) primarily by the wardens *hospitaleros* in the pilgrim hostels but also in cathedrals, churches, hostels, bars and town halls along the way. ***You need 2 stamps per day from Sarria.***

You may be able to obtain a pilgrim passport before travelling from a local Confraternity (see useful addresses at the back) just be sure to apply in good time. Alternatively you can obtain a *credencial* on arrival at the pilgrim office in Santiago or Sarria. Though every effort should still be made to join and support the work of the Confraternities who do so much to prepare and maintain the route and its facilities.

ACCOMMODATION: Pilgrim hostels: *albergues de peregrinos* vary in what they provide but lodging is usually in bunk beds with overflow space on mattresses *colchonetas*. Number of beds and dormitories are shown in brackets *[8÷2] -v- [40÷1]* (to provide an idea of density!) + private rooms *+4*. Xunta/ municipal hostels provide a kitchen with basic cooking equipment and a dining / sitting area. Opening times vary but most are generally cleaned and open again from early afternoon (13:00). You cannot reserve a bed in advance in Xunta hostels and phone numbers are provided for emergency calls or to check availability outside the normal seasons (most are open between April and October but can close for holidays or maintenance purposes).

Hotels •*H* Number of rooms is shown (*x2* versus *x102*) gives an idea of the atmosphere and likely facilities on offer. Hostales •*Hs*, pensiónes •*P* or casa rurales •*CR* literally 'rural house' (a type of up-market B&B) vary widely from €30-€90 depending on season and the facilities offered. Where a price range is shown in this guide the lower price is based on one person per night *individual* and the higher for 2 people sharing *double*.

Closures: While there is always a chance businesses will close, the recent pandemic and the economic repercussions of this have exacerbated the situation. Any accommodation recently reported as closed is marked in ***black*** as opposed to **pink**, but has been left in the guide in case the closure is temporary. If you plan on staying in any accommodation marked as currently closed please check for updates.

Costs: Some parish and monastery hostels still work on a donation basis *donativo* and, unless we find ourselves destitute, we should try and leave at least €5 for a bunk bed and use of a hot shower. Allow for a basic *minimum* €30 a day to include overnight stay at a Xunta hostel (€10) and remainder for food and drink. Some hostals provide a communal dinner (dependent on the warden *hospitalero*) and most have a basic kitchen *cocina* where a meal can be prepared. Alternatively most locations have one or more restaurants to choose from. Pilgrim menus *menú peregrino* are generally available for around €9 incl. wine. If you want to indulge in the wonderful seafood *mariscos* available in Galicia and accompany this with the delightful local *Albariño* wines expect to treble the basic cost!

Ⓐ Albergues fit into 6 main categories – the shortened form appears on the maps e.g. Private *Priv. Prices can change at short notice and are provided as a guide only. Some include breakfast and this is shown as € incl.*

❶ Xunta & Municipal *Xunta. & Mun.* Basic hostels owned and maintained by the Galician government (Xunta) or local (Municipal) authority with average cost €10. The warden *hospitalero/a* often lives on site or near by.

❷ Parish *Par.* hostel *albergue parroquia* these are generally owned by the local diocese. Some offer a regular pilgrim mass and they tend to be more informal and relaxed than municipal hostels with a communal meal and blessing. Generally welcoming but basic, €7+ often by donation *donativo*.

❸ Convent or Monastery *Conv.* hostel *monasterio o convento* (*mosteiro* in Gallego) *Convento* on its own is a monastery (monks) while *convento de monjas* (nuns) is a convent! The atmosphere in each is often markedly different so check the details provided (av. cost €7+ or *donativo*).

❹ *Asoc.* **Association** hostels are owned and run by local Spanish or other national confraternities, sometimes in conjunction with the local authority. They tend to be particularly well equipped for the needs of the pilgrim and are generally staffed by former pilgrim volunteers (av. cost €12+).

❺ *Priv.**(star) **Network** hostels **Red de Albergues** are private hostels that have formed themselves into a loose association. They are often owned and maintained by an individual but are increasingly being handed over to a management group. They have a similar sense of brotherhood/sisterhood as in confraternity hostels but often provide additional facilities (av. cost €12+).

❻ *Priv.* **Private** hostel *albergue privado* with no overall code or regulations they tend to be more flexible (commercial realities) with a full range of facilities and more flexible opening hours as well as the option to book in advance. Expect to pay €12+ (additional private rooms + from €30).

SAFETY: The camino offers a remarkably safe environment in an arguably unsafe world. Incidents of theft are rare but occur the world over, especially in larger towns and cities where the disparity between rich and poor is most noticeable. Likewise theft from hostels is rare but has been known to occur.

Trust in God but tether your camel seems like sensible advice.

Major roads and fast traffic are a safety concern and great care is advised on stretches of the route that cross roads or run parallel to main roads. Every effort has been made to minimise these and to offer alternative options but some encounters with traffic are unavoidable so stay present and alert when interacting with cars.

When viewed in a global context few cases of hostile behaviour or harassment are reported on the camino but have been known to occur. It is wise to be cautious when travelling alone especially in the evening or at night. Many people choose to walk the camino alone, but due to the moving community of pilgrims we are rarely truly alone. If you ever feel nervous or unsafe consider keeping a group of pilgrims in sight, or asking to walk with someone until you feel comfortable again. We have a wonderful opportunity as pilgrims travelling together to support and look out for each other and to keep each other safe. In the event of an emergency or to report an incident use the EU emergency number **112**. The Spanish Police (Guardía Civil) have also released an app, AlertCops (which can be downloaded from your app store) this allows you to send an alert or report an incident directly from your smartphone and also includes a location sharing feature.

MOBILE PHONES: Along with a steep increase in pilgrims on the camino in recent years there has also been a dramatic rise in mobile phone use*. This constant connectivity with our familiar *outer* world can keep us disconnected from the expansiveness of our *inner* world. This disconnect is multi-layered. It can diminish  our relationship to each passing moment, the camaraderie of our 'camino family' and the connection to our divine essence. Finding the courage to face our fears and step outside our comfort zone can lead us to Self-discovery. This may require limiting our dependency on external aids. Imagine who we might meet in the space created by letting go of these distractions? Most of us will carry a mobile phone for practical or safety reasons but we might consider limiting its use and being aware of how/when we use it.

*Anthropologist Nancy Louise Frey, PhD, author of Pilgrim Stories (see bibliography) researches the impact of the Internet Age on the camino. Her website *www.walkingtopresence.com* explores how our tech habits can limit the power of the pilgrim experience and offers tips on how to deepen our connection to the inner journey.

OPENING TIMES: The culture of *siesta* affects the opening times of many businesses which close during the middle of the day, particularly in rural areas. Tourist offices and museums are generally open from 10:00–13:00 and again after *siesta* from 16:00–19:00. Shop hours are generally a bit longer. *Note:* that many public buildings, including churches, are **closed on Mondays**.

RESPECTING NATURE: Please don't leave waste behind you. Orange peel can take 20 years to decompose; plastic bottles 500! Collect some rubbish along the way each day with the intention of leaving the path *better* than you found it. If a sense of superiority arises, visualise yourself cleaning up the mess that you left behind at other times in your life when you were, perhaps, less aware. Pilgrims are not hikers *per se* and many will not be familiar with the  country code. Human waste is a particular problem so check out café stops for toilet breaks and discipline your bowels. It only takes a few unaware pilgrims to create the problem... and only a small band of conscientious ones to inform and help alleviate it. You might also like to try a psychic cleansing after experiencing any negativity in your own thoughts or in any interaction that you witness that are unkind. Simply shake out the negativity from your mind and invite loving thoughts to replace them. These simple practises will help to keep both the physical and psychic environments clean and unpolluted.

RESPECTING FELLOW PILGRIMS: Facilities such as showers and kitchens have a limited supply of hot water and utensils and these, especially during the summer months, can be stretched. Be aware of your own needs but also of the needs of others and try and find a balance that feels right. If you have arrived early and bagged the best bed keep an eye on who comes in later – if you are on a bottom bunk and someone arrives late with a damaged knee could you move to a top bunk? Observe your reactions but don't judge yourself. There is already enough guilt in the world to engulf it and we certainly don't need more! Awareness is the starting point for change.

PREPARATION - *OUTER:*

Physical Preparation – what shape is my body in? Any reasonably fit person can accomplish this journey without undue stress. I walked from Seville to Santiago (1,000+ km) with a grandfather who celebrated his 80th birthday en route. 94 is the most senior pilgrim I have met so far! However, if you have recently had an illness or are otherwise concerned about your state of health then do have a medical check up. It may take time to adjust to walking with full backpack. Give body, mind and soul time to acclimatise and don't push yourself on the early stages.

Training: It is always advisable to put in some physical training before you go. I would be surprised if more than 10% of pilgrims actually act on this advice. If you are one of the 90% who haven't then *please* heed the advice to take the first few days slowly. Lightweight walking poles, if used properly, can greatly reduce wear and tear on the body. Using one in each hand creates better balance and is twice as effective.

Bag Weight: A related matter is the weight you carry in your backpack. The more additional weight you carry the more pressure on your body. Aim to carry no more than 10% of your body weight with an ***upper limit of 10 Kilos (22 lbs)***. Remember the weight of food and water will be added to whatever you pack! Pilgrimage is a great metaphor for life. What are you carrying that is not really necessary? The following kit lists may help you reduce your luggage to what is truly essential and remember...

"From contentment with little comes happiness." African proverb.

EQUIPMENT AND CLOTHING: *Think quality not quantity*

Your pilgrimage starts at the planning stage. So start by invoking the highest intention for your journey and bring awareness to what you buy. There is so much exploitation of human and natural resources supported by our unconscious consumerism. Become informed and use your voice and money to support those companies who genuinely try to make a positive difference in the world or consider buying second hand. To walk a pilgrim path for peace in gear produced from exploitative business practises or oppressive regimes is not congruent – we must make every effort to *walk our talk*.

What to bring? You will bring too much; everyone does!

Whatever you carry your knees and feet will absorb most of the shock and will be the first to buckle if you carry more than essentials. Buy materials that are essentially: (a) lightweight and non-bulky (b) that wick away moisture from your skin (c) are easy to wash and quick to dry.

Essential equipment:

○ **walking shoes / boots:** should provide good ankle support, be breathable, lightweight and yet have strong soles for the rough ground you will encounter. Heavyweight boots are not necessary but consider trail shoes with waterproof lining if travelling in the winter season. **Sandals** or lightweight shoes for use in the evening will give your walking shoes time to dry out and give your feet a chance to breathe.

○ **socks:** bring several pairs as it is a good idea to change socks and massage your feet half-way through the day (even if you don't think they need it).

○ **trousers, skirts and shorts:** for most of the year shorts are ideal and your legs will dry out much more quickly than fabric if you walk into a rain shower. Rural Spain remains very traditional – a sarong is ideal to wrap around bare legs when visiting churches, etc., and also cool and easy to wash and dry.

○ **fleece:** a lightweight fleece is useful – you will need to increase the thickness the closer into winter that you plan to travel. If you intend travelling in mid-winter you will need proper thermal clothing and a sleeping bag for the subzero temperatures that you may encounter, particularly on the higher ground where you can expect snow and ice.

○ **waterproofs:** even allowing for obvious seasonal changes the weather in northern Spain, particularly in Galicia, is notoriously unpredictable. There are many lightweight rain and wind-proof jackets and trousers, though they can be expensive. A cheaper option is a plastic poncho that covers not only the body but the backpack as well. This can be rolled out during rain showers and the loose fitting nature of the poncho means you don't get *too* much build up of sweat as with most tight-fitting plastic or nylon garments. Ponchos are readily available online and due to popularity may be found in pilgrim shops en route.

○ **hat:** in the summer months your main consideration will be protection from the sun. A wide brim hat can protect your head and neck. Sunstroke can be painful and, in extreme cases, dangerous.

○ **rucksack:** 50 litres should be ample, avoid a large capacity rucksack (70 +litres) as you may be tempted to fill it with unnecessary items. An essential element is the waist strap that must allow you to adjust and carry the weight on your hips – *not* your shoulders. Using dry bags inside your rucksack will ensure dry kit at the end of a wet day. If you are not using a poncho then a backpack cover is also recommended for heavy downpours.

○ **sleeping bag:** essential for all pilgrim hostels. If you are travelling in the summer months a lightweight 1 or 2 season bag will suffice (or just a sheet bag). A zip will allow you to open it up in very hot conditions. Most hostels, especially in the mountain areas, have blankets.

○ **toiletries:** Apart from the usual take small scissors, needle and thread for draining blisters and essential repairs.

○ **water container: Water is essential** and evidence supports the view that a minimum 2 litres a day can significantly reduce fatigue, blisters and other common ailments of long distance walking as well as avoiding dehydration. There are drinking fonts *fuente* [⛲] all along the way – fill up at every opportunity  especially in high summer when drinking fonts can dry up. Non-tap water is often OK to drink but not guaranteed *sin garantia* – check with locals if in doubt. You may notice a difference between the quality of water around the main cities with their chemical additives, so empty and refill from the purer waters of the mountains and rural villages whenever possible.

○ **first aid/ medication:** All hostels are obliged to carry first aid boxes and there are innumerable chemists *farmacia* along the way. However, some essentials should be carried with you. Consider plasters and antiseptic ointment for cuts and pain relief tablets such as Paracetamol for toothache etc. and Ibuprofen for relief of muscular pain. Bring a high factor sun protection and apply regularly. Also consider lip protection and after sun lotion. Elasticised tubing can help support a sprained knee or ankle.

Be sure to bring an adequate supply of any prescribed medication, e.g. Inhalers for asthmatics, as these may be difficult to obtain en route without prescription.

○ **Blisters:** While prevention is better than cure, unless you are a well seasoned walker you will get blisters! Each to their own, but *Compeed* is readily available, easy to apply and acts as a second skin. Whatever you bring apply it as soon as you feel a hot spot developing (don't wait until it has developed into a full blister). Many make the mistake of loosening shoes to relieve the pressure but this can aggravate the friction – the cause of the problem in the first place. Make sure your footwear fits snugly.

○ **Homeopathy:** For the Homeopathically inclined essentials might include: Arnica for muscular sprains and bruising, Calendula for cuts and Combudoron for insect bites. For those using chemically based products, bring equivalent treatments.

Optional Extras:

○ **walking poles:** while not essential, they are highly recommended and will greatly reduce the impact on your body, around 25% if used properly, e.g. taking the strain on the strap, don't clutch with your fingers (use blister pads if necessary). They will steady you over rough patches and may create confidence when passing barking dogs. Take two to avoid becoming lopsided. Most pilgrims opt for a wooden staff collected along the way and that is certainly better than nothing.

○ **sleeping mat:** useful if you want the freedom of experiencing life under the stars or if you are travelling in the busy season as it allows you more options – there will always be a floor somewhere! *Therm-a-Rest* or similar offers good comfort but is more expensive than a basic foam-style mat.

○ **cooking utensils:** many hostels have basic kitchen equipment and creating a meal is a great way to bond with other pilgrims and keep costs down. If you intend cooking regularly it is advisable to bring your own utensils.

○ **camping equipment:** there is no need to carry a tent; however, if you enjoy and are experienced in the outdoors you will know what to bring. Campsites en route are few and far between and few hostels have facilities for tents.

○ **books:** be *very* selective as books add enormously to weight and you may be surprised how little time you have for reading. Historical notes and more detailed information on the many artistic treasures to be found along the way are often issued free of charge from tourist offices or as part of the price of an entry ticket.

A CHECKLIST with Spanish translations is provided to help strengthen your vocabulary and assist you to buy or replace items along the way. This is not necessarily a recommended list, as this will vary depending on individual need and through the seasons.

Clothes:	*Ropas:*
hat (sun)	*sombrero*
sunglasses	*gafas de sol*
shirt(s)	*camisa(s)*
T-shirt(s)	*camiseta(s)*
jacket –	*chaqueta –*
waterproof	* chubasquera*
breathable	* transpirable*
underpants	*calzoncillos*
shorts	*pantalones cortos*
trousers	*pantalones largos*
socks	*calcetines*

Shoes:	*Zapatos:*
boots (mountain)	*botas (de montaña)*
shoes (walking)	*zapatos (de andar)*
sandals (leather)	*sandalias (piel)*

Size:	*Tamaño:*
larger	*mas grande*
smaller	*mas pequeño*
cheaper	*mas barato*
more expensive	*mas caro*

Essential documents	*Documentos esenciales:*
passport	*pasaporte*
pilgrim record	*credencial de peregrino*
wallet / purse	*monedero / cartera*
cash	*dinero en efectivo*
credit card	*tarjeta de crédito*
travel tickets	*pasaje de viaje*
daily	*diario*
emergency addresses	*dirección de emergencia*
phone numbers	*números de teléfono*

Backpack	*Mochila*
rain cover	*protección de mochila*
sleeping bag	*saco de dormir*
towel	*toalla*
water bottle	*botella de agua*
penknife	*navaja*
torch	*linterna*

Toiletries:

soap
shampoo
tooth brush / toothpaste
hair brush
sink stopper
shaving cream
razor (blades)
face cloth
sun cream (lotion)
after sun cream
moisturiser
toilet paper
tissues
sanitary pads
tampons

First Aid Kit:

painkiller
aspirin / paracetemol
plasters
blister pads
compeed-*second skin*
antiseptic cream
muscular ache (ointment)
homeopathic remedies

Medicine (prescription):

asthma inhaler
hay fever tablets
diarrhoea pills

Accessories: (optional)

walking poles
pilgrim shell
wrist watch
alarm clock
poncho
sleeping mat
clothes pegs
clothes line (cord)
earplugs (against snoring)
mug / cup
cutlery
knife
fork
spoon

Artículos de tocador:

jabón
champú
cepillo de dientes / dentífrico
cepillo de pelo
tapón de fregadero
espuma de afeitar
maquinilla de afeitar
guante de aseo
crema solar (loción)
leche solar (after sun)
crema hidratante
papel higiénico
pañuelos de papel
salva-slips
tampones

Botiquín

analgésico
aspirina / paracetamol
tiritas
apósito para ampollas
compeed-segunda piel
crema antiséptica
(pomada) dolores musculares
remedios homeopáticos

Medicina (prescripción):

inhalador para el asma
medicina para las alergias
pastillas para la diarrea

Accesorios: (opcional)

bastones de caminar
concha de peregrino
reloj de pulsera
despertador
poncho
esterilla
pinzas para la ropa
cuerda para tender ropa
tapones para los oídos (ronquidos)
taza / vaso
cubiertos
cuchillo
tenedor
cuchara

Language *Lenguaje:*
The Spanish are proud of their national identity and language, particularly in rural areas. It is a matter of extreme discourtesy to assume that everyone will automatically speak English. To walk into a shop or to stop and ask directions in anything other than the native language of the area you are travelling through is clearly insensitive. It behoves pilgrims to have at least a few basic phrases and to make the time to learn and use them. English is *not* widely spoken in the countryside. Ideally get a language CD a month or two *before* you travel and spend a few minutes each day practising this lovely lyrical language – the third most widely spoken in the world. Be sure to take a small dictionary and phrase book with you. Below you will find some basic pilgrim words and phrases that may not be included in a general phrase book.

As all place names and directions will, of course, be in Spanish (or Galego as we are in Galicia) all maps have been prepared accordingly. Some common phrases and words have also been scattered around the text as a reminder that you are a guest in someone else's country. For the real novice, I have included words that have a similar resonance between English and Spanish. This should enable you to more readily bring to mind the required word, even if it isn't exactly *exactamente* the word that a professional translator might have used. An example is vigilance! with the Spanish counterpart ¡*Vigilancia*! One might more properly use the word danger *peligroso* but this bears no resemblance to the English word at all. For those of you who are *elocuente*, please *omitir* the following *sección*! Spanish is placed in italics immediately following the English word or phrase.

Nouns are gender specific. Words ending in *e* are (generally) masculine and those in *a* feminine. Plural (generally) add *s* or *es* at end of the word *el* or *la*, *los* or *las*; the man *el hombre,* the men *los hombres,* the woman *la señora,* the women *las señoras.*

Vowels are always articulated; **a** pronounced (pron:) as in far; **i** as in deed; **e** as in bed; **o** as in obey; **u** as in food. **Emphasis** is on the penultimate syllable Melide, pron: Meh-**lee**-deh; unless denoted with an accent; Nájera, pron: **Ná**-kher-a, *not* Ná-**kher**-a.

Consonants are similar to English excepting: 'c' pron: th as in then. Centre *centro* pron: **then**-*tro* - 'd' at the end of a word is pron: th as in path. You *usted,* pron: *oo-***steth**. Note here the emphasis is on the last syllable, an exception to the rule! – 'g' and 'j' have a guttural kh sound similar to a Scottish loch: urgent *urgente* pron: *er-***khen**-*tay* or garden *jardín* pron: *khar-***deen** (note emphasis on last syllable because it has an accent) – 'h' is always silent. Hotels *hoteles* pron: *oh-***tel**-*es*. – 'll' is pronounced with a lyeh sound / full *lleno* pron: **lyeh**-*no*. – 'ñ' is pron: as in onion / tomorrow *mañana* pron: *man-***yahn**-*ah*. – 'qu' is pron: as in k for key / fifteen *quince* pron: **keen**-*thay*. – 'v' falls between v and soft b sound / journey *viaje* pron: *bhee-**a**-khay*. 'X' in Galego as 'sh' / Xunta pron: Shunta. 'Z' as in 'th' / Zumo pron: thoomo.

Verbs are more complex but follow 3 basic forms: [1] those ending in *-ar* as in *hablar* to speak. I speak *hablo*, you speak *hablas*, he/she speaks *habla*, we speak *hablamos*, you all speak *habláis,* they speak *hablan*. [2] those ending in *-er* as in *comer* to eat. I eat *como*, you eat *comes*, he/she eats *come*, we eat *comemos*, you all eat *coméis*, they eat *comen*. [3] those ending in *-ir* as in *vivir* to live. I live *vivo*, you live *vives*, he/she lives *vive*, we live *vivimos*, you all live *vivís*, they live *vivan*. Use the irregular verb 'to go' for the future tense. I am going to mass tomorrow *Voy a misa mañana*. We are going to León *Vamos a León*.

Basic Phrases: so here are a few simple phrases to get you going. A new language can't be learnt in a day; but it is really important that you *try* whenever the opportunity arises – everyone loves a trier.

Greetings / *Saludos*
Yes / *Sí*   No / *No*
Please / *Por favor*   Thanks / *Gracias*

How are things? / *Qué tal?*   Have a good trip / *Buen viaje*
Hello! How are you? / *Hola! Cómo está?*
Good day / evening / night *Buenos días / Buenas tardes / Buenos noches*
Goodbye! Until later / *¡Adiós! Hasta luego*

Welcome / *Bienvenida*
What's your name? / *¿Cómo se llama?* My name is ... / *Me llamo ...*
Where do you live? / *¿Dónde vives?* I live in London / *Vivo en Londres*
Are you English? / *Es usted Inglés?* I'm Irish / *Soy Irlandes(a)*
I'm single / *Estoy soltero(a)* I'm married / *Estoy casado(a)*
I have 2 sons / *Tengo dos hijos(as)* I have no children / *No tengo hijos*
I'm here on (pilgrimage) / *Estoy aquí de peregrinación*

Excuse me! / *¡Disculpe!*   **Pardon? / *¿Perdone?***
What did you say / *¿Cómo dice?*   It's not important / *No importa*
Do you understand? / *¿Entiende?*   I don't understand! / *¡No entiendo!*

I speak very little Spanish / *Hablo muy poco español*
Do you speak English? / *¿Habla usted Inglés?*
How do you pronounce that? / *¿Cómo se pronuncia eso?*
Please write it down. / *Escríbamelo, por favor*
What does this mean? / *¿Qué significa esto?*

Where is it? / *¿Dónde está?*
Here / *Aquí*   There / *Allí*
On the left / *a la izquierda*   On the right / *a la derecha*
Outside the bank / *Fuera del banco*   Beside the cafe / *Al lado del café*
Near the centre / *Cerca del centro*   Opposite / *Enfrente...*
Where are you going? / *¿A dónde vas?*

Where is the pilgrim hostel / *¿Dónde está el albergue de peregrinos?*
Where are the toilets / *¿Dónde están los servicios?*
Where can I change some money? / *¿Dónde se puede cambiar dinero?*
Where do I get the taxi to the airport? / *¿Dónde se coge el taxi al aeropuerto?*
How do I get to the centre of León? / *¿Cómo se va al centro de León?*

What time is it? / *¿Qué hora es?*

It's midday / *Es mediodía*
Ten past two / *Son los dos y diez*
Quarter to six / *seis menos cuarto*
Today / *Hoy*   Yesterday / *Ayer*
Day after tomorrow / *Pasado mañana*
Last week / *la semana pasada*
Next year / *al año que viene*

Five past one / *Es la una y cinco*
Half past three / *Son las tres y media*
Five to seven / *siete menos cinco*
Tomorrow / *Mañana*

This month / *este mes*
Every year / *todos los años*

What day is it today? / *¿Qué día es hoy?*

Lunes / Martes / Miércoles / Jueves / Viernes / Sábado / Domingo
What is today's date? / *¿Qué fecha es hoy?*
It's April 10th / *Estamos a diez de abril*

spring / *primavera*   **summer / *verano***
autumn / *otoño*   winter / *invierno*
*enero / febrero / marzo / abril / mayo / junio / julio / agosto / septiembre /
octubre / noviembre / diciembre*

Room / *Habitación*

Do you have any vacancies? / *¿Tienen alguna habitación libre?*
I'd like a room for one night / *Quería una habitación para una noche*
There's a problem with the room / *La habitación tiene un problema*
It's too hot (cold) / *Hace demasiado calor (frío)*
There is no hot water / *No hay agua caliente*
Where can I wash my clothes / *¿Dónde puedo lavar mi ropa?*

Doctor / *Médico*   Dentist / *Dentista*

I need a dentist (doctor) / *Necesito un dentista (medico)*
Where is the health centre? / *¿Dónde está el centro de salud?*
I have blisters / *Tengo ampollas*
I have tendinitis / *Tengo tendinitis*
My leg/knee/foot/toe...hurts / *Mi pierna/rodillo/pie/dedo del pie...me duele*
My ankle is swollen / *Mi tobillo está hinchado*
My lower back is in spasm / *Mi espalda tiene una contractura*
Where is the pharmacy? / *¿Dónde está la farmacia?*

Food / *Comida*   Menu / *Menú*

breakfast / *desayuno*   lunch / *la comida*
savoury snack / *tapas*   dinner / *cena*
meat / *carne*   **fish / *pescado***

beef steak / *bistec*
fillet steak / *filete*
pork / *cerdo*
lamb / *cordero*
veal / *ternera*
chops / *chuletas*
ham / *jamón*
chicken / *pollo*
vegetables / verduras
desert / *postre*
sandwich / *bocadillo*
I am hungry / *Tengo hambre*

trout / *trucha*
salmon / *salmón*
sole / *lenguado*
hake / *merluza*
prawns / *gambas*
squid / *calamares*
mussels / *mejillones*
seafood / *mariscos*
(tomato) salad / ensalada (de tomate)
fruit / *fruta*
cheese / *queso*
I am thirsty / *Tengo sed*

red wine / vino tinto
water / *agua*

white wine / vino blanco
milk / *leche*

What time is dinner (breakfast) / *¿A qué hora es la cena (el desayuno)?*
Is there a vegetarian restaurant? / *¿Hay un restaurante vegetariano?*
What's today's special / *¿Cuál es el plato del día?*
Do you have a menu in English / *¿Tiene un menú en Inglés?*

Train / Tren
Have you a timetable?
What time do we get to León?
How much is a single (return) ticket?
I want to cancel my reservation
When does the museum open?
When does the bus arrive at Arcos?
When is the next train to Bilbao?

Bus / Autobús
/ *¿Tienen un horario?*
/ *¿A qué hora llegamos a León?*
/ *¿Cuánto cuesta un billete de ida (y vuelta)*
/ *Quería anular mi reserva*
/ *¿Cuándo abre el museo?*
/ *¿Cuándo llega el autobús a Arcos?*
/ *¿Cuándo sale el próximo tren para Bilbao?*

Shoes / Zapatos
I take size 8 / *Calzo el cuarenta*
footwear / *calzado*
shoemaker / *zapatero*

Size / Talla

shoelace / *el cordón*
shoeshop / *zapatería*

Clothes / Ropa
I take size 40 / *Mi talla es la 40*
Have you a bigger (smaller) size? /
big / *grande*
(See under check list for other items)

Size / Talla

Tiene una talla mas mayor (menor)
small / *pequeño(a)*

Books: (limited)
phrase book –
  Spanish
  French
post office / *Correos*

Libros: (cupo lim.)
libro de frases –
  Español
  Francés
Stamps / *Sellos*

• Megalithic period c. 4000 B.C.E

History tells us little about the Neolithic peoples who inhabited the western fringes of Europe. However, evidence of their stonework can be found all over the Galician landscape and goes back at least 6,000 years as seen in the petroglyphs and rock art of 4,000 B.C.E and the dolmens *mamoas* of the same period. These mega-monuments are dotted all around Galicia. This megalithic culture was deeply religious in nature and left a powerful impact on the peoples who followed.

• Early Celtic period c. 1000 B.C.E

Central European Celts settled in western Spain inter-marrying with the Iberians. These Celti-Iberians were the forebears of the Celtic Nerios peoples who came to inhabit Galicia centuries before the Roman occupation. Remains of their Celtic villages *castros* can still be seen around the remote countryside. These fortified villages were built in a circular formation usually occupying some elevated ground or hillock. The extensive mineral deposits of Galicia gave rise to a rich artistic movement and Celtic bronze and gold artefacts from this area can be seen in museums all across Europe.

Galicia remains one of the least well known of the Celtic nations and yet it is one of the oldest. Galician Celts trace their mythic lineage to the king of Scythia in the Black sea area where the Druid Caichar had a vision in which he saw them travelling west to found Galicia and Ireland. The first Gaelic colony was established in Galicia under Brath and his son Breogán the latter becoming the legendary hero who founded Brigantium (present day A Coruña) entering folklore and the national anthem of Galicia in the process, *'Wake up from your dreams, home of Breogán.'* His grandson became King Milesius after whom the Celtic Milesians were named. It is generally accepted that the first Celts to settle in Ireland were Milesians from Galicia. In a masterful stroke of genius early Christian monks then extended the Celtic lineage 36 generations back to link it with the biblical Adam!

• Early Christian Period c. 40 C.E.

While there is no historical evidence to support the view that St. James preached in Galicia, there are some anecdotal references to that effect. *(see photo of Santiago Peregrino from the parish church in Finisterre. This church also has a statue of Christ much revered in Galicia and associated with many miracles).* It would appear that St. James sailed to Galicia, probably Padrón, to preach Christ's message, his body being brought back there after his martyrdom in Jerusalem around 40 C.E It is reasonable to assume that he, or his followers, would have sought to bring the Christian message to areas of spiritual significance on which to graft its own message. Finisterre was one of the most significant spiritual sites in the world at that time and it was inevitable that it would draw those with a spiritual mission. It was also accessible, being directly on the sea route from Palestine. However, sea routes were not the only ways to access this corner of the world and Roman roads were being built that linked Portugal and Spain to France and the rest of Europe.

• *Early Roman period 100 B.C.E*

By the end of the first century the Romans controlled most of the southern Iberian peninsular naming the unruly northern province Hispania Ulterior to include the area known as Gallaecia. In 61 BC Julius Caesar became governor and conducted naval expeditions along the coast and finally wrested control of the Atlantic seaboard from the Phoenicians. In 136 the proconsul Decimus Junius Brutus led his legions across the Lima and Minho rivers to enter Gallaecia for the first time. He met resistance not only from the fierce inhabitants but also from his own soldiers wary of crossing the river Lima thought to represent one of the rivers of Hades – the river of forgetfulness Lethe. Brutus became

the first Roman general to make it to Finisterre 'by road' and was reputedly mesmerised at the way the sea 'drank up' the sun and was predisposed to the pagan and Druidic worship centred on the Phoenician Altar to the Sun Ara Solis. The photo (right) shows Cabo Da Nave in the background that was said to represent a Roman Centurion at death facing west to the 'Land of Eternal Youth' Tir-na-Nóg).

• *The Middle Ages 476 – 1453*

Hispania was the Latin name given to the whole Iberian peninsula. After the fall of the Roman Empire in 476 C.E. the north-western province (present day Galicia) was ruled by the Vandals, Suevi and Visigoths, descendants of the Germanic tribes that had overrun Roman Hispania leading to its collapse. It is hard to believe (and little understood) that the Moorish 'invasion' of the Iberian peninsula in 711 was actually an invitation to the forces of Islam by the squabbling Visigoth nobles to help in their domestic feuds. The Umayyad Muslims were happy to oblige and so the invasion by invitation began. Muslim forces quickly moved north to conquer the whole peninsular, capturing the bells of Santiago cathedral along the way and infamously taking them to Granada. But Galicia proved impossible to control and Islamic rule here lasted only a few decades. It was to take another 700 years before the re-conquest was complete in the south – and the bells returned to Santiago.

Even the briefest sketch of Spanish history would not be complete without looking at the contribution of the Templar knights both to the reconquest reconquista of the Iberian peninsular from Islamic rule to Christianity but also its subsequent support of the pilgrimage routes to (and from) Santiago. These warrior monks originated in Jerusalem in 1118 B.C.E. with a vow to 'protect pilgrims

on the roads leading to Jerusalem'. Their headquarters were located in part of the original Solomon's Temple or Temple Mount. After the Holy Land was 'lost' to Islam the whole centre of focus was switched to the reconquest of Spain. This is when the image of St. James the Moor-slayer Santiago Matamoros first appeared on a white charger to spearhead the reconquista. Behind this powerful and terrifying image of St. James with the slain moors at his feet (see photo) came the Knights Templar mounted on their own chargers and dressed in their familiar white tunics emblazoned with the Templar Cross.

Once the reconquest was complete the Knights switched their role to protecting the pilgrim from other perils of the road. In 1307 the French monarch Philippe IV moved against the Knights in an attempt to purloin their considerable fortunes to alleviate his own financial problems and the Order 'blended' into the Hospitallers.

• The Catholic Monarchs 1469 – 1516

The marriage in 1469 of Isabella I of Castille and Fernando II of Aragón saw the merging of two of the most powerful kingdoms in Spain. The title Catholic Monarchs *los Reyes Católicos* was bestowed by Pope Alexander VI with an eye to aiding the re-conquest and unifying Spain under Roman Catholicism. This was finally achieved after the conquest of the Muslim Kingdom of Granada in 1492, the same year Columbus 'discovered' the Americas. This illustrious period was tarnished by the expulsion or massacre of non-Catholics under the infamous Inquisition initiated under her reign. Isabella is, perhaps, best remembered for her more beneficent activities such as the building of the pilgrim hospital in Santiago, now the luxurious parador Hostal Dos Reis Católicos – reputedly the oldest hotel in the world in continuous occupation for that purpose.

• The War(s) of Independence 1807 – 1814

Despite its remote location, Galicia was not spared the effects of the War of Independence 'Peninsular War' (1807–1814) when forces of Napoleon ransacked many of the villages we pass through. This was a military conflict between Napoleon's empire and Bourbon Spain for control of the Iberian

Peninsula during the Napoleonic Wars. It began when the French and Spanish invaded Portugal in 1807 and escalated the following year when France turned on its former ally Spain and lasted until Napoleon was defeated in 1814. The Peninsular War overlaps with the Spanish War of Independence *Guerra de la Independencia Española* which began with the uprising on 2 May 1808 *Dos de Mayo* (still remembered today in many a street name).

• *The Carlist Wars & First Spanish Republic 1833 – 1876*

The Carlist Wars followed between followers of Carlos V and his descendants fighting for absolutist Monarch supported by the Catholic church against the forces of liberalism and republicanism. Towards the end of the 3rd Carlist war the first Spanish Republic was proclaimed in 1873. Again the remoteness of Galicia was no bar to its involvement in anti-monarchist activities. Indeed its resistance to any outside interference continues to this day.

No introduction to Galicia would be complete without mention of Castelao who was born in Rianxo in 1886 and who died in Buenos Aires in 1950. Politician, writer, and doctor. Identified as a founding father of Galician nationalism, identity and culture and president of the Galician Gelegust Party. He presented the idea of an independent Galician State *Estatuto de Galicia* to the Spanish Parliament in the same year that General Franco appeared on the political scene. Despite various initiatives to earn independence for Galicia it was not until 1981 that it achieved a measure of autonomy, being recognised as a separate autonomous region in that year. A footnote to his life suggests that he was a convinced pro-European. He wrote in *Sempre en Galiza* that one of his dreams was to, 'see the emergence of a United States of Europe'.

• *The Spanish Civil War 1936 – 1939 & Franco Period.*

In 1936 General Franco seized power leading to one of the bloodiest civil wars in history and its effects can still be felt today despite the 'Pact of Forgetting' *Pacto del Olvido*. This was a decision by all parties to the conflict to avoid dealing with the horrifying legacy of Fascism under Franco. The Pact attempted to transition from an autocratic to democratic rule of law without recriminations for the countless thousands killed summarily and buried in unmarked graves throughout Spain. While suppression of painful memories helped in national reconciliation at that time – these memories remain close to the surface. There is a growing body of opinion within Spain today that it should now take a more honest and open look at the violence of that period. The Spanish Civil War *Guerra Civil Española* pitted Republicans (with Communist and Socialist sympathies), against the Nationalists a predominantly conservative Catholic and Fascist grouping led by General Francisco Franco. Fascism prevailed not least owing to the intervention of Nazi Germany and Fascist Italy who provided weapons, soldiers and air bombardment (Guernica). This struggle between democracy and fascism for the soul of Spain was to last until Franco's death in 1975.

• *Galicia Today 1975 – today*

After Franco's death King Carlos nominally succeeded and appointed political reformist Adolfo Suárez to form a government. In 1982 the Spanish Socialist Workers' Party *Partido Socialista Obrero Español* **PSOE** won a sweeping victory under Felipe González who successfully steered Spain into full membership of the EEC in 1986. In 1996 José María Aznar, leader of the centre-right People's Party *Partido Popular* **PP** won a narrow mandate but in 2002 the oil tanker Prestige ran into a storm off Finisterre and the ensuing ecological catastrophe sank not only the livelihood of scores of Galician fisherman but, in due time, the right wing government as well resulting in a popular cry up and down the country of 'never again' *nunca maís*. With the socialist's back in power under José Luis Rodríguez Zapatero the government set in motion an immediate change in foreign policy and, more controversially, a sudden but decisive shift from a conservative Catholic to a liberal secular society that led to one newspaper headline, *'Church and State square up in struggle for the spirit of Spain.'* ... The fine balance between secular and religious Spain and the alliances and coalitions between the socialist and conservative parties in government continue yet, seemingly immune to all these social and political upheavals, the *Caminos* go quietly about their gentle spirit of transformation.

Galician Culture: The flowering of Galician art that took place under Alfonso VII and Ferdinand II (kings of Galicia until it was absorbed into León and Castille under Ferdinand III) saw the completion of the great cathedrals of Ourense, Lugo and Tui, as well as Santiago. However, between the three great powers comprising the Catholic monarchy, the Aristocracy and Castille; Galician art, culture and language were greatly diluted. Indeed while the French Way *Camino Francés* introduced wonderfully inspiring European art and artisans to towns all along the route to Santiago, it had the effect of diminishing the Celtic influences within Galicia.

Galician Language: The distinctive language of Galicia *Gallego* is still widely used today. The language institute estimates that 94% of the population understand it, while 88% can speak it. Gallego belongs to the Iberian Romance group of languages with some common aspects with Portuguese. Phrase books between Spanish *Castellano* Galician *Gallego* and English are difficult to find but one of the more obvious differences is the substitution of the Spanish J – hard as in Junta (pron: **kh**unta) as opposed to the softer Galego Xunta (pron: **sh**unta). Here are a few common phrases to help distinguish one from the other:

The Jacobean Way	*Del Camino Jacobeo*	*Do Camiño Xacobeo*
Fountains of Galicia	*Las Fuentes de Galicia*	*Das Fontes de Galiza*
The Botanical garden	*El Jardin Botanico*	*O Xardín Botánico*
Collegiate church	*Colegiata Iglesia*	*Colexiata Igrexa*
Below the main Square	*Bajo el plaza mayor*	*Debaixo do praza maior*

The Revival *Rexurdimento* of Galician language and literature in the XIX[th]C was spearheaded with the publication in 1863 of *Cantares Gallegos* by the incomparable Galician poetess, Rosalía Castro. The Revival reached its zenith in the 1880's with the publication of many illuminating Galician texts such as *Follas Novas* also by Rosalía Castro, *Saudades Galegas* by Lamas de Carvajal and *Queixumes dos Pinos* by Eduardo Pondal. Galicia's culture has been kept alive as much by its exiles, political and economic, as by those that remained behind. The unofficial anthem of Galicia, The Pines *Os Pinos* was written and first sung in South America where it urged the Galician people to awaken from the yoke of servitude into freedom: *'Listen to the voices of the murmuring pines which is none other than the voices of the Galician people.'* However, even the pine trees seem under threat from the imported eucalyptus that has taken over large swathes of the countryside.

The fruits of this revival can be tasted, nonetheless, throughout Galicia today. You may well hear the swirl of the traditional Galician bagpipes *Gaita* in the bars of Santiago or at one of its many festivals and fairs that take place throughout the year. Many of these are based on the ancient Celtic celebration of the seasons particularly at the equinoxes and the summer and winter solstices. The short pilgrimages to local shrines *romerías* endorse the deeply held religious values of the people of Galicia but drawing ever larger crowds are the secular festivals such as the Night of the Templars *Noche Templaria* which is, in fact, a 5 day celebration of traditional markets, parades, music events and firework shows.

Galician Nationalism appears to be born more out of a deep pride in its traditions, rather than a need to overthrow a culture that has been imposed from outside. This is not unlike other Celtic cultures that have found themselves marginalised on the Western fringes of Europe. We demean Galicia and ourselves by stereotyping popular Spanish culture onto her. This is not the Spain of castanets, paella and Rioja wines. Her identity is clearly Celtic with *gaitas, mariscos* and *Albariño* wines predominating – all of which are a cause of justified pride.

SELF-ASSESSMENT *INNER WAYMARKS*

This self-assessment questionnaire is designed to encourage us to reflect on our life and its direction. We might view it as a snapshot of this moment in our evolving life-story. In the busyness that surrounds us we often fail to take stock of where we are headed. We are the authors of our unfolding drama and can re-write the script anytime we choose. Our next steps are up to us...

We might find it useful to initially answer these questions in quick succession as this may allow a more intuitive response. Afterwards, we can reflect more deeply and check if our intellectual response confirms these, change them or bring in other insights. You can download copies of the questionnaire from the *Camino Guides* website so that you can repeat the exercise on your return and again in (say) 6 months time. This way we can compare results and ensure we follow through on any insights and commitments that come to us while walking the camino.

☐ How do I differentiate pilgrimage from a long distance walk?
☐ How do I define spirituality – what does it mean to me?
☐ How is *my* spirituality expressed at home and at work?

☐ What do I see as the primary purpose of my life?
☐ Am I working consciously towards fulfilling that purpose?
☐ How clear am I on my goal and the right direction for me at this time?
☐ How will I recognise resistance to any changes required to reach my goal?

☐ When did I first become aware of a desire to take time-out?
☐ What prompted me originally to go on the Camino de Santiago?
☐ Did the prompt come from something that I felt needed changing?
☐ Make a list of what appears to be blocking any change from happening.

☐ What help might I need on a practical, emotional and spiritual level?
☐ How will I recognise the right help or correct answer?
☐ What are the likely challenges in working towards my unique potential?
☐ What are my next steps towards fulfilling that potential?

How aware am I of the following? (score on a level of 1 – 10)
Compare these scores again on returning from the camino.

☐ Clarity on what inspires me and the capacity to live my passion
☐ Confidence to follow my intuitive sense of the 'right' direction
☐ Ability to recognise my false egoic guide and the 'wrong' direction
☐ Ability to recognise my resistances and patterns of defence
☐ Ease with asking for, and receiving, support from others
☐ Awareness of my inner spiritual world

REFLECTIONS:

"I am doing the camino once again, looking for something I left behind or perhaps never found. It's like coming home." Notes of a pilgrim from New Mexico.

What are *my* reflections? Why am *I* walking the camino?

_____

_____

_____

_____

_____

_____

_____

_____

_____

_____

_____

_____

_____

_____

_____

_____

_____

_____

_____

_____

_____

_____

_____

_____

This guidebook provides you with essential information in a concise format. The maps have been designed so you can instantly see how far it is to the next place of interest without having to scale the distance. Distances on the maps correspond to those in the text and are generally spaced at around 3 km intervals (approximately 1 hour of walking at an average pace). For clarity and accuracy each stage begins and ends at the front door of a specified pilgrim hostel or other defined 'end point'. Maps are one directional *to* Santiago; if you intend to walk the route 'in reverse' source conventional maps. The camino path is shown as follows:

❶ ● ● ● ● **Main Route** (carrying around 80% of pilgrims) generally follows the most direct path and is indicated by a line of yellow dots symbolic of the yellow arrows / shells that will be your guide throughout the journey. Distances along this route are shown in **blue.**

❷ ● ● ● ● **Scenic Routes** are generally not waymarked on the ground but provide a "greener" alternative to the main route. These quieter paths are shown with **green** dots indicating the natural landscape they travel through. Any text appears on a green panel.

❸ ● ● ● ● **Detours** to places of special interest are shown with **turquoise** dots and the text appears on a turquoise panel.

❹ ● ● ● ● **Road Routes** follow on or close to asphalt roads and are marked with **grey** dots symbolising asphalt.

❺ ● ● ● ● **Alternative Route** via a point of religious significance (eg. monastery) shown in **purple**.

Waymarks: Thanks to the voluntary efforts of various associations and 'friends of the way' – waymarking is now so thorough that we need only the barest information to get us safely to the end of each stage. These signs come in a variety of forms - see some examples of the familiar yellow arrows *flechas amrillas* below. If you get 'lost' it is invariably because you have let your mind wander and your feet have followed! – stay present and focused especially at points shown with an exclamation mark [**!**]. If you find yourself temporarily off-course be careful when asking directions as locals are not always familiar with the waymarked paths and may direct you along the public roads – it is often best to re-trace your steps until you pick up the waymarks again.

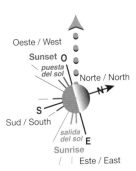

A **Sun-Compass** has been provided on each map as an aid to orientation. Should you become 'lost' this will help re-orientate. Even in poor weather we can generally tell the direction of the sun so, for example, if you are walking from Sarria to Portomarín you are heading west and the morning sun will be at your back (east). At midday the sun will be to your left (south) and by late afternoon you will be walking towards the sun (west). If you find yourself in the late afternoon with the sun on your back – stop and re-assess.

Distances:: Each day's stage is measured from the front door of one albergue to the next, i.e. daily distances are between sleeping accommodation. The maps have been designed to show relevant information only and are therefore not strictly to scale – instead accurate distances are given between each point marked on the map and this corresponds to the text for ease of reference. Distances in between these points are shown bracketed in the text as follows: [1.0 km] plus [0.2 km] add up to the boxed figure in blue `1.2 km` .Villages in Spain, particularly Galicia, tend to straggle without any defined centre and even the local church is frequently located outside the actual town. Distances are usually measured to the albergue or other clearly defined feature.

Language: Text and place names are provided in *Galego* unless they appear 'on the ground' in Spanish. The Church of St. John may, therefore, appear as *Iglesia San Juan* or *Igrexa San Xoán*.

Contour Guides are shown for each day. This will give you a thumbnail sketch of the day's terrain and help you prepare for the uphill stretches and anticipate the downhill ones. They are drawn to an exaggerated scale to emphasise steep inclines.

Abbreviations: The following abbreviations are used throughout the text:

<left means *turn* left – (left) means *on* your left. right> *turn* right etc.

s/o = continue straight on
c. = circa (about)
c/ = Calle
🍴 = Restaurant
XIIᵗʰc / 12ᵗʰ century.
[?] indicates an option.
[!] = Attention! Indicates dangerous road / steep descents / poor waymarking.

adj. = adjoing / adjacent
incl. = including
r/ = Rua
V. = Vegetarian
[m] mobile phone number
[⛲] *fuente* drinking font.

Accommodation pricing: €pp = per person / incl. = including breakfast)
€25 – 40 = price for single room – price for double room.

Distance and Pace: Many pilgrims are not hikers *per se* so the following chart can help establish the reasonable distance you can accomplish each day. Helping you to avoid arriving at your destination *before* you are ready to stop or struggling to reach it at the end of a long day.

You also need to adjust your time depending on the *cumulative* ascent. This 'additional' time is given for each stage and is based on the Naismith rule of 10 minutes for every 100 metres climbed. A cumulative ascent of 900m = 90 minutes or *±1½ hrs*. Remember *steep* descents (as opposed to gradual) also slow pace and most injuries (sprains and strains) are sustained going *down*hill.

Fitness Level	kph	minutes/km	20km	25km	30km	35km
			The above distances (kilometres) will take the following time (hours)			
Fast walker	5 kph	12 min's/km	4.0	5.0	6.0	7.0
Average pace	4 kph	15 min's/km	5.0	6.3	7.5	8.6
Leisurely pace	3 kph	20 min's/km	6.6	8.3	—	—

Our pace depends on many other factors, apart from gradient. Time of day and so heat is important as this has the biggest effect on speed and endurance. Ideally start each day early and either (a) finish by lunchtime or (b) plan a midday stop, rest in the shade, and continue on when the worst heat of the day is over.

End of day pace will produce the biggest variations. On the longer stretches you may find your pace slowing considerably and you should allow half the normal pace (double the time) at the end of a long day. Bare this in mind when deciding whether to continue onwards after a long day. *Pilgrims tend to only query* **distances** *for the last section of a day that they feel must be longer than that published! That is why it is misleading to publish* **time** *rather than distance for any section.*

> While our maps are presented in daily stages please do not feel under any pressure to stick to these. Numerous alternative accommodation is listed so we strongly advise you to plan daily stages and distances that work for *you*.

Traversing cities. Waymarking in cities has to compete with advertising, traffic lights and other distractions, so allow time to retrace steps if you take a wrong turning.

Traffic can be dangerous and draining. The main (N-*National*) roads are shown in red, symbolic of their added danger and volume of traffic. Every effort has been made to minimise exposure to these 'red' routes and extra care is needed on the few stretches where they simply cannot be avoided. [!] .

Senda: These modern gravel paths offer a practical but somewhat soulless addition to the camino. They generally run alongside and parallel to the public road with the consequent noise but are relatively safe and soft underfoot.

PREPARATION – A Quick Guide:

❶ Before you go

• **When?** (see p.7) Spring can be wet and windy but the route is relatively quiet with early flowers appearing. Summer is busy and hot and hostels often full. Autumn can provides stable weather with harvesting adding to the colour of the countryside. Winter is solitary and cold, some hostels will be closed.

❷ Preparation – *Outer*: what do I need to take *and* leave behind (see p.16)
• Buy your boots in time to walk them in before you go.
• Pack a Poncho, Spain can provide downpours at any time of year.
• Bring a hat, sunstroke is painful and can be dangerous.
• Look again if your backpack weighs more than 10 kilos.

... *and* consider leaving behind.

• Books, except this one – all the maps you need are included.
• Don't take 'extras' Spain has shops if you need to replace anything.
• Everything that is superfluous for pilgrimage. Take time to reflect carefully on this point as it can form the basis of our questioning of what is really important in our life and spiritual awakening. We have become reliant, even addicted, to so many extraneous 'things'. We need to de-clutter in order to clear space for what truly matters to arise in our awareness. Being fully present to each passing moment is to free the mind from constant connectivity with the digital universe and its web of distractions.

❸ Language learn it now, *before* you go (see p.22).

❹ Pilgrim Passport, protocol & Prayer
• Get a *credencial* from your local confraternity – and join it (see p.91).
• Have *consideration* for your fellow pilgrims and gratitude for your hosts.
• May every step be a prayer for peace and an extension of loving kindness.

❺ Safety (see p.14) The camino offers a remarkably safe environment in an inherently unsafe world - but accidents and crime happen. In the event of an emergency the EU wide emergency number is **112**.

❻ Preparation – *Inner*: why am I doing this? (see p.32)
Take time to prepare a purpose for this pilgrimage and to complete the self-assessment questionnaire. Start from the basis that you are essentially a spiritual being on a human journey, not a human being on a spiritual one. We came to learn some lesson and this pilgrimage affords an opportunity to find out what that is. Ask for help and expect it – it's there, now, waiting for you.

Whatever you do – for heaven's sake don't forget to start.

Preparation Notes:

Total km *equiv.*	Total distance for stage Adjusted for cumulative climb (each 100m vertical +10 mins)
(850m) **Alto** ▲	Contours / High point of each stage
< Ⓐ Ⓗ >	Intermediate accommodation ➲ (*often less busy / quieter*)
3.5 ►	Precise distance between points (3.5 km = ± 1 hour)
–● 50m > / ^ / <	Interim distances 50m right> / s/o=straight on^ / <left

,,,,,,,,,,,,,,,,,,,,,,	Natural path / forest track / gravel *senda*
▬▬▬▬▬	Quiet country lane (asphalt)
▭▭◎▭▭	Secondary road (*grey*: asphalt) / Roundabout *rotonda*
▬N-11▬	Main road [N-] *Nacional* (*red*: additional traffic and hazard)
▬A-1▬	Motorway *autopista* (*blue*: conventional motorway colour)
++++++++●	Railway *ferrocarril* / Station *estación*

● ● ● ● ● ●	Main Waymarked route (*yellow*: ± 80% of pilgrims)
● ● ● ● ● ●	Alternative Scenic route (*green*: more remote / less pilgrims)
● ● ● ● ● ●	Alternative road route (*grey*: more asphalt & traffic)
● ● ● ● ● ●	Optional detour *desvío* (*turquoise*: to point of interest)
● ● ● ● ● ●	Primary Path of pilgrimage (***purple***: inner path of Soul)

Ⓧ ❓ ❶	Crossing *cruce* / Option *opción* / Extra care *¡cuidado!*
↑ ⚶ ↑	Windmill *molino* / Viewpoint *punto de vista* / Radio mast
▪━▪/▪━▪	National boundary / Provincial boundary *límite provincial*
∼/∼	River *río* / Riverlet Stream *arroyo* / *rego*
◯/	Sea or lake *Mar o lago* / Woodland *bosques*
♁ ♦ †	Church *iglesia* / Chapel *capilla* / Wayside cross *cruceiro*

⊕ 🍺 ⚲	Drinking font *fuente* [⚱] / Café-Bar ☕ / Shop (*mini*)*mercado* 🛒
¶ *menú* V.	Restaurant / *menú peregrino* / V. *Vegetariano(a)*
ℹ 🏠 ✕	Tourist office ➊ *turismo* / Manor house *pazo* / Rest area *picnic*
✚ ✚ ✉	Pharmacy *farmacia* / Hospital / Post office *correos*
✈ 🚉 ⛽	Airport / Bus station *estación de autobús / gasolinera*
⁑ *XIIc.*	Ancient monument / 12th century

Ⓗ Ⓟ Ⓒ	Hotels •*H-H˙*€30-90 / Pension •*P˙*€20-35 / •*CR (B&B)* €35-75
x12 €35-45	Number of private rooms *x12* €35(single)-45 (double) *approx*
Ⓗ Ⓐ Ⓐ	*Off* route lodging / Ⓐ Reported closed - check for updates
Ⓐ❶❷ Ⓙ	Pilgrim hostel(s) *Albergue* ●*Alb.* + Youth hostel ●*Juventude*
[32]	Number of bed spaces (usually bunk beds *literas*) €5-€17
[÷4] +12	÷ number of dormitories / *+12* number of private rooms €30+

Par.	Parish hostel *Parroquial* donation *donativo* / €5
Conv.	Convent or monastery hostel *donativo* / €5
Mun/Xunta	Municipal hostel €5+ / Galician government *Xunta* €8
Asoc.	Association hostel €8+
Priv. (*)	Private hostel (network*) €10-17
	[*all prices average (low season) for comparison purposes only*]

p.55	Town plan *plan de la ciudad* with page number
(Pop.– Alt. m)	Town population – altitude in metres
▭	City suburbs / outskirts *afueras* (*grey*)
▭	Historical centre *centro histórico / barrio antiguo* (*brown*)

Welcome to Galicia!

O Cebreiro provides a wonderful foretaste of the distinctive Galician culture that now awaits. The mountains of Galicia are the first object in 5,000 km that the westerly winds across the Atlantic hit so you can expect an immediate change in weather with frequent rain showers and thunderstorms *chubascos y tormentas* and thick mountain fog *niebla* all feeding a maze of mountain streams and deep river valleys. The countryside is reminiscent of other Celtic lands with its small, intimate fields and lush pastures grazed by cattle with sheep, pigs, geese and chickens all foraging amongst the poorer ground. Thick hot soups *caldo gallego* and rich vegetable and meat stews provide inner warmth from the damp. Local red wines with their coarser characters accompany most meals and help to fuel the inner glow. Nearer the coast, fish dishes such as steamed octopus dusted with paprika *pulpo a la galega* and shellfish *mariscos* will dominate. To accompany scallops *vieiras* try the white Ribeiros or the incomparable Albariño wine. Round off your meal with local cheese and quince jelly *queso y membrillo* or the famous almond tart *tarta de Santiago.* If you are still feeling cold, try the distilled grape skin *orujo* or its marginally less alcoholic and more refined cousin *hierbas* mixed with local herbs. Stone granaries *hórreos* are everywhere storing the local harvest, primarily maize *maíz,* out of reach of rat and rain.

Galicia also shares many historical similarities with other Celtic regions like the west of Ireland. Too poor to provide much employment for its large family structures, emigration (particularly of the younger men) has cast its spectre across the region. Here, women drive the tractors or herd the oxen and seem to find time to do the cooking and tend the bars as well. Surprisingly you may find locals who speak good English on account of having spent time working abroad (or while visiting children working in the UK or USA). If any doubt remains as to its Celtic past then the strident whirl of its bagpipes *gaita* should dispel them. The language *Galega* is still spoken by a substantial minority and understood by the majority while poets such as Rosalia de Castro have helped preserve it more robustly than Irish or Scottish Gaelic. The most visible difference is in the spelling of place names and signposts where, for example, X (Sh...) replaces J (Kh...) as in Xunta (Shunta) Xardín etc. Galicia bids you One Hundred thousand welcomes *Céad míle fáilte!*

Galicia's material poverty has left her with an abundance of spiritual wealth and the region is generally at peace with itself and its traditions largely intact. While a strong Catholic faith overlays its earthy spirituality, its pagan past never totally faded. Deep respect for, even veneration of, the natural elements remains as evident as the elements themselves. *Finis terra* was, after all, the end of the ancient world – west of Finisterre was the 'Land of Eternal Youth' *Tir-na-nog* where the sun never set. Long before the tomb of St. James was discovered and before Christianity spread to these shores, pilgrims from all over the known world came here to witness the sun sink in the west – and to open to some transcendental reality that emphasised the temporal aspects of this earthly life.

The countryside ahead is full of the megalithic burial mounds *dolmens* and *mamoas* of these earlier settlers who were deeply reverent in character and who handed down this earthy respect for the natural world. The wayside crosses *cruceiros* add an air of solemnity to the path and are a reminder of the deep spirituality of Galicia that seems to have survived the consumer culture and materialism that has swept over much of the rest of Europe. Santiago is the capital of the autonomous region of Galicia that is divided into the 4 provinces of A Coruña, Lugo, Ourense and Pontevedra. See *A Pilgrim's Guide to Camino Finisterre* for a detailed account of the history and legends of this fascinating corner of Galicia – and try and make time to walk the route out to the end of the *way* and the world.

In 2016 the government *Xunta* started replacing the concrete bollards *mojón* with *historico* (main camino) and *alternativo* (routes to 'historical' sites not directly en route!). Adding to the confusion they are updating the original distances which had become out of date. However, the route is constantly changing so it is best to use these bollards for directional purposes only.

O CEBREIRO (Pron: *oh-thay-bray-***air**-*oh*) is a significant gateway on the camino and has ministered to pilgrims since the twilight of the first millennium. ***Santa María la Real*** is patroness of the area and her XII[th]c statue is prominently displayed along with the chalice and paten connected with the miracle of O Cebreiro *Santo Milagro in which, 'a haughty celebrant' of the mass, dismissive of a devout and humble peasant, saw the bread and wine turn into the body and blood of Christ as he offered them to the supplicant who had risked life and limb to attend mass in a terrible snowstorm. The statue itself was also said to have inclined its head at the miraculous event.'*

This hilltop village is home to the oldest extant church associated directly with the pilgrim way dating from the IX[th]c. The Cathedral Chaplaincy Outreach will welcome pilgrims (in English) during the day followed by an international Pilgrims' Mass in the evening. The church also marks the final resting place of ***Don Elias Valiña Sampedro*** (1929–1989 – see photo above) the parish priest who did so much during his lifetime to restore and preserve the integrity of the camino. It was his idea to mark the route with the familiar yellow arrow ➡ and it was largely as a result of his efforts that we walk the route today, he was also the inspiration behind the caminoguides. His bust presides over the church square and many confraternities have placed their names on the plinth as a mark of their deep respect for his life and efforts on behalf of the modern pilgrim. He was also responsible for the restoration of the adjoining Hostal *San Giraldo de Aurillac* that is now run by members of the family. These handsome stone buildings originally formed part of the monastic settlement dating back to the XI[th]c when King Alfonso VI assigned their care to the monks of the Abbé de Saint Giraldo from France. Queen Isabella stayed here in 1486 on her pilgrimage to Santiago. Opp. the church is a museum in a renovated Palloza.

Albergues: ❶ **Casa Campelo** *Priv.* *[10÷1]* €15 *+4* €50 ℂ 982 179 317. A 200m walk past the bars, shops and restaurants takes us to ❷ **O Cebreiro** *Xunta.* *[104÷2]* €10 ℂ 660 396 809 on the western (far) end of the village on an exposed and elevated site above the main road (see photo>). This purpose built hostel with all facilities provides lodging for 104 people in over two dormitories.

Other Lodging: •*H* O Cebreiro *x5* €40-50 ℂ 982 367 182 *www. hotelcebreiro.com* with ❙/*bar* adj. church & souvenir shop + San Giraldo de Aurillac ℂ 982 367 125. •*CR* **Navarro** *x3* €30-45 ℂ 982 367 007 *casaturismoruralnavarro.com/en/.* •*Hs* **Mesón Antón** *x4* €60+ ℂ 982 151 336 +❙ •*P* **Casa Carolo** *x10* €40-48 ℂ 982 367 168. •*CR* **Venta Celta** *x5* €45+ ℂ 667 553 006 +❙ •*CR* **Casa Valiña** *x5* €40-50 ℂ 982 367 125. •*CR* **Casa Frade** *x5* €43 ℂ 982 367 104.

O Cebreiro is a popular tourist venue as well as pilgrim halt – demand for beds can outstrip supply in the summer which can, in some cases, lead to high prices and low standards. Find a bed before celebrating your arrival and note that additional lodging can be found in Pedrafita O Cebreiro 4.5 km. *off* route. Monbus *www.monbus.es/en* now operate a daily service to/from Santiago to Pedrafita stopping at most of the villages en route (all 61!).

Personal Reflections:

01 O CEBREIRO – TRIACASTELA
Santiago – 156.8 km (*97.4 ml*)

▦▦▦▦▦	--- ---	19.7 --- ---	95%
▬▬▬▬	--- ---	1.0 --- ---	05%
▬▬▬▬	--- ---	0.0	
Total km		**20.7** km (*12.9 ml*)	

◣◣ Total ascent **410**m ±¾ *hr*
***Alto.**m* ▲ Alto do Poio **1,335**m (*4,380 ft*)
<▣ ▥> ➲Liñares **3.1** km ➲Hospital **5.6**
➲Alto do Poio **8.6** km ➲Fonfría **11.9** ➲ Biduedo **14.3** ➲Filloba **17.4** km.

The Practical Path: While this stage is only 20.7 kms and mostly downhill, most injuries are sustained going down (not up) so extra care is needed. There are several villages and drinking fonts along the way and splendid views in every direction (weather permitting). Early morning mists can give rise to amazing ethereal *floating islands* where hilltops appear above the clouds. These exotic experiences generally give way to clearer skies, as the sun burns the early morning mists away. Whatever time of year, be prepared for *any* weather, as Galicia, particularly the mountain areas can be very unpredictable.

The Mystical Path: High places help lift us towards Higher Mind. At such heights, a wider perspective opens up to both the physical and the inner eye. What do you see, feel and hear from this elevated space? Do the angels incline their heads to listen to your prayers? Does the silence and peace in your heart allow the inner voice to be heard? Are you open to receiving a miracle and to seeing the inner rainbow – symbol of God's Covenant? *If you want the rainbow, you gotta put up with the rain. Dolly Parton.*

Personal Reflections: *"... The deluge continues and not a break to be seen in the clouds in any direction. I ask myself was it serendipity that sent the brief shaft of light through the tiny church window bathing me in its warm rich glow; its light so strong I was momentarily dazed by it. I sense again that altered state, devoid of ego, and all the pain of yesterday has gone. I feel inspired to write a pilgrim guidebook and Don Elias Valiña Sampedro appears to have given me his authority and blessing and so I commit to the Call of the Camino; right here and now ..."*

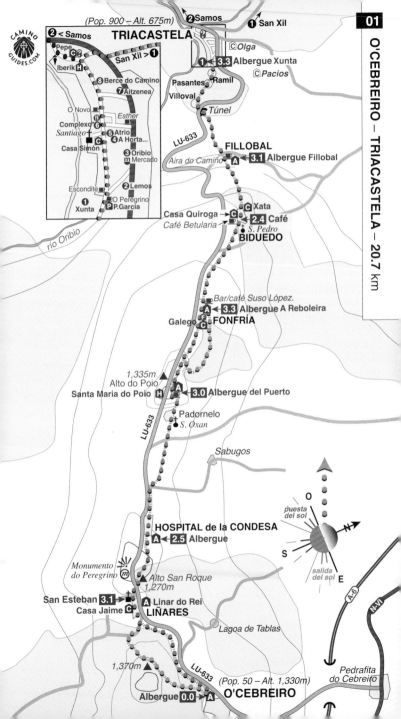

CAMINO
GUIDES.COM

2 Samos   **1** San Xil

(Pop. 900 – Alt. 675m)
2 < Samos
TRIACASTELA
Pepe **C** ♦ 🅿
Iberik **H**
San Xil > **1**

🅒 *Olga*
1 **3.3** Albergue Xunta
🅒 *Pacios*

Pasantes   Ramil
Villoval

8 Berce do Camino
7 Aitzenea
O Novo
Esther
Complexo 🏨 **6**
Santiago† **5** Atrio
Casa Simón 🅒 **4** A Horta...
3 Oribio
🅜 Mercado
Escondite 🅟 **2** Lemos
🅟 O Peregrino
1 Xunta 🅟 P.Garcia

🅒 *Túnel*

LU-633
FILLOBAL
Aira do Camiño **A** **3.1** Albergue Fillobal

🅒 Xata
Casa Quiroga → 🅒 **2.4** Café
Café Betularia 🅒 † S. Pedro
BIDUEDO

río Oribio

Bar/café Suso López.
A **3.3** Albergue A Reboleira
Galego 🅒 **FONFRÍA**

1,335m
Alto do Poio
Santa Maria do Poio **H** **A** **3.0** Albergue del Puerto

LU-633
† Padornelo
S. Oxan

Sabugos

HOSPITAL de la CONDESA
A **2.5** Albergue

O
puesta del sol
N
S
salida del sol E

Monumento do Peregrino 🅜
🔆 Alto San Roque
1,270m
San Esteban **3.1** †
Casa Jaime 🅒   **A** Linar do Rei
LIÑARES

Lagoa de Tablas

A-6
N-VI

1,370m ▲
LU-633
(Pop. 50 – Alt. 1,330m)
Albergue **0.0** → **A** **O'CEBREIRO**

Pedrafita do Cebreiro

0.0 km O Cebreiro *Albergue* Take lower track parallel to road or ●●● alt. forest path that winds around the hill above, reaching a high point in Galicia at 1,370m. It then drops down to join the main route in Linares, thus avoiding the track alongside the main road (see map previous page).

3.1 km Liñares small hamlet that once grew flax *lino (Linares)* for the linen trade. ●*Alb.* Linar do Rei *Priv.[20÷4]* €12 +*1* €40 ℂ 616 464 831 (Erica). •*CR* Casa Jaime *x4* €40 ℂ 982 367 166 🍴 *bar.* Pass the ancient parish church of San Esteban VIII[th]c. Shortly afterwards we cross the road onto track up to *Alto de San Roque* [**1.0** km] where an statue of a medieval pilgrim looks out over the expanse of Galicia and its deep valleys (see photo previous page). Path continues parallel to the road for [**1.5** km] into:

2.5 km Hospital de la Condesa ●*Alb.* Xunta.*[18÷2]* €10 ℂ 660 396 810 located above the road (right) as we enter the village. •*CR* O Tear *x2* €30 ℂ 982 367 183 with 🍴🍴🍴. The village once boasted a pilgrim hospital (hence its name) and was reputed to have been one of the earliest ever built for Christian pilgrims on the way to Santiago. The pre-Romanesque *Iglesia St Juan XI[b]C* (also dedicated to San Roque) has a delightful interior and unusual stone roofed belfry and cross of Santiago aloft. The track continues parallel to the main road turning off right> [**1.2** km] down a minor road (signposted Sarbugos) for [**0.3** km] before picking up a path into Padornelo [**1.0** km] with the restored chapel *ermita San Oxan* connecting this area with the Order of St. John. A short but steep climb brings us to another high spot on the camino in Galicia 1,335m. (4,380 feet) [**0.5** km]:

3.0 km Alto do Poio ●*Alb.*del Puerto *Priv.[18÷1]* €6 +*4* €25 ℂ982 367 172 adj. Bar Puerto caters for a brisk breakfast trade with pilgrims from O Cebreiro. On the opp. side of the road •*Hs* Santa María de Poio *x20* €40 ℂ 982 367 167. Join track parallel to the road. [●●● *After 400m* **option** *turn sharp right for alterative 'green' route that rejoins main path into Fonfria].*

3.3 km Fonfría typical Galician village •*P* Casa Lucas *x3* €40+ ℂ 690 346 740 *www.casadelucas.es* and •*CR* Núñez *x2* €45 ℂ 982 161 335 🍴🍴🍴. Fill your flask from the cool waters *fons fría* [🚰] after which the hamlet is named. At the far end of the village is ●*Alb.* A Reboleira *Priv.***[50÷2]* €8 +*8* €40+ ℂ 982 181 271 mod. building with adj. palloza. Menú €9. Adj. 🍴🍴🍴 *Suso López.* S/o track parallel to main road and turn right> into:

2.4 km Biduedo rural idyll *capilla de San Pedro Meson Betularia* adj.•*CR* Quiroga *x9* €40 ℂ 982 187 299 (Celia). Also •*CR* Xata *x7* €24-36 ℂ 982 189 808. The path now begins to descend steeply with wonderful views over the countryside to the west. Next we arrive at crossroads and rest area:

3.1 km Fillobal ●*Alb.* Fillobal *Priv.[18÷2]* €12 +*2* €40 ℂ 666 826 414 adj. 🍴 *Aira do Camino.* S/o over country lane down steeply on path across main road (muddy underpass) through *As Pasantes* [**1.4** km] and *Ramil* [**1.7** km] on the ancient camino worn down with the feet of countless pilgrims and local livestock, a classic stretch of *corredoira* (narrow lane walled-in with granite). Meander above the wooded valley of the arroyo Roxino that flows down from Monte Oribio. Oak and chestnut trees offer shade into **Triacastela [0.2** km]:

3.3 km Triacastela *Alb.* ❶ Xunta *[56÷14]* €10 green-field site to left of the camino at the start of the village overlooking the river. Stone buildings with modern glazed extension and outdoor recreation area. Opp. popular ⫲/☛ *O Peregrino* (evening sun) and adj. •*P'* **García** *x3* €40 Ⓒ 982 548 024. The ramp up at the side of bar connects to the main road and ultra modern *Alb* ❷ **Lemos** *Priv.[12÷1]* €10 *+10* €43 Ⓒ 677 117 238 www.pensionalberguelemos. com and ❸ **Oribio** *Priv.[27÷2]* €10 Ⓒ 982 548 085 with all facilities. Continuing down c/del Peregrino (*right – access also off main road*). •*P'* **Casa Simón** *x4* €40+ Ⓒ 982 548 438. ❹ **A Horta de Abel** *Priv.[14÷2]* €11 *+3* €40 Ⓒ 608 080 556. •*P'* **Casa Simón** *x4* €40+ on corner (*left*) *Igrexa de Santiago* to rear adj. ❺ **Atrio** *Priv.[20÷3]* €10 *+6* €40 Ⓒ 982 548 488 (Juan José). ❻ **Complexo Xacobeo** *Priv*.*[36÷3]* €11 *+12* €40 Ⓒ 982 548 037 with all facilities, adj. ⫲/☛ *Xacobeo* (same ownership). This marks the central 'hub' of town. •*Hs* **O'Novo** Ⓒ 982 548 105. Further on (*right*) slip road to ❼ **Aitzenea** *Priv.[38÷4]* €9 Ⓒ 982 548 076 www.aitzenea.com. Sympathetic conversion of traditional stone house (*aitzenea is Basque for stone-house*). At the end of town (700m from entrance) we find: ❽ **Berce do Camiño** *Priv. [28÷6]* €9 Ⓒ 982 548 127 all facilities in modernised terraced house adj. Caixa Galicia. •*H'* **Iberik** *x16* €44+ Ⓒ 982 650 061 www.iberikhoteles.com opp. •*P* **Casa Pepe** *x6* €50 Ⓒ 622 084 338 **Other Lodging:** •*P''* **Casa David** *x7* €40 Ⓒ 982 548 105 and •*Hs* **Mesón Vilasante** *x12* €35-45 Ⓒ 982 548 116. •*CR* **Olga** *x4* €40+ Ⓒ 982 548 134 c/ Castro 2 (+0.5 km). •*CR* **Pacios** €35+ Ⓒ 982 548 455 Vilavella (+ 2.0 km). ☛ *Esther* Rúa Peregrino. *[Next albergue: Route* ❶*A Balsa (1.6 km) Route* ❷ *Lusio (4.5 km [400m off route])*

TRIACASTELA town of the *three castles* none of which survive and an important stop for medieval pilgrims coming down off the mountain with several hospices and an extensive monastery. XI stage in the Codex Calixtinus. It is no less an attractive stop today with a wide selection of bars, restaurants and hostels serving the increasing number

of pilgrims passing through. The parish church is dedicated to Santiago and has an unusual XVIII[th]C tower on which is carved a relief of the three castles (see photo). Pilgrim mass daily at 18:00, *every*one welcome by the delightful Fr. Augusto. Nearby are the quarries that provided the limestone used in the building of Santiago Cathedral. Medieval pilgrims would carry as much as they were able to the lime kilns in Casteñeda (through which we pass during stage 05) and the pilgrim monument in the lower town square recognises this ancient tradition while acknowledging the rebirth of the camino – paying equal respect to both.

02 TRIACASTELA – SARRIA
Santiago – 136.1 km (*84.6 ml*)

....	--- ---	11.2 --- ---	*60%*
─────	--- ---	7.5 --- ---	*40%*
▬▬▬	--- ---	0.0	
Total km		**18.7** km (*11.6 ml*)	

Total ascent **230m** ±½ hr
Alto.m ▲ Alto Riocabo **905m** (*2,970 ft*)

< Ⓐ Ⓗ > ❶ ● *San Xil:* ↪Ⓐ Balsa **1.6** ↪Pintín **12.1** km ↪ Calvor **13.4** km ↪San Mamed **14.8** km ↪Vigo de Sarria **17.7** km
❷ ● *Samos:* ↪*Lusío* **5.1** *km* (+ 0.4) ↪ Samos **10.5** ↪ San Mamed **21.4** km

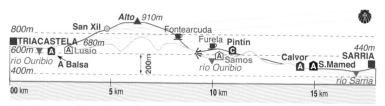

The Practical Path: Before leaving Triacastela decide whether to take northern **direct route** ❶ *via San Xil* ●●●● (18.7 km) or the southern **detour route** ❷ *via Samos* ●●●● (25.5 km). Improvements to the San Xil route (new woodland paths) have increased the natural pathways to 60%. It is 6.4 km shorter than the route via Samos and has the steep climb up to alto do Riocabo with splendid views. The road route to Samos has sections along the busy LU-633 which can be dangerous. (*The criterion used in this guide is to always favour natural pathways*). The Benedictine monastery of Samos is one of the oldest and largest in Spain and draws large tourist numbers. Both routes are attractive and offer good alternative accommodation:

The Mystical Path: Will the winding river reveal her natural weir to you? The man-made example, which diverts water to the village mill in San Cristobo, is no match for the beauty of this one. The unadorned beauty of this path remains largely undiscovered by officialdom. How long will it remain in its pristine state uncluttered by the trappings of man? ***Happiness is a mystery, like religion, and should never be rationalised.*** G.K. Chesterton

Personal Reflections "... *The deepening silence coupled with a rare break in the downpour mingle with the glorious Landscape Temple to create an overwhelming sense of wellbeing. I am entirely alone and yet I feel more connected to a larger Way than at any other time in my life.*

0.0 km Triacastela from albergue ❶ proceed to the far end of town and until the option point where you have a choice of routes:

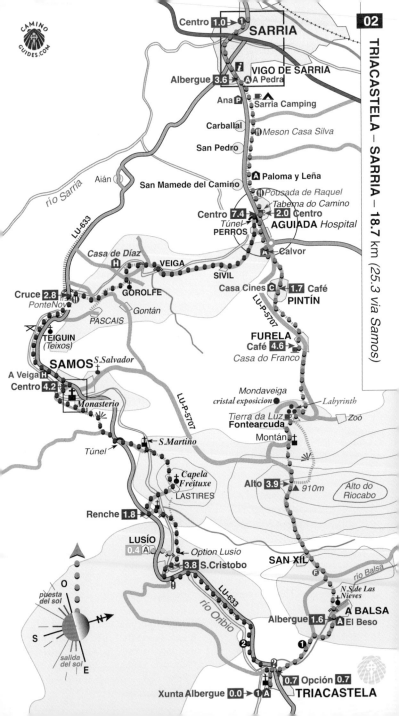

CAMINO
GUIDES.COM

Centro **1.0** → **1** SARRIA

i VIGO DE SARRIA

Albergue **3.6** → **A** A Pedra

Ana **P** **🏕** Sarria Camping

Carballal **🍴** Meson Casa Silva

San Pedro

San Mamede del Camino

rio Sarria

Aián

A Paloma y Leña

🍴 Pousada de Raquel
Taberna do Camino

Centro **7.4** → **2.0** Centro AGUIADA Hospital
Túnel
PERROS
A → Calvor

LU-633

Casa de Díaz
H → VEIGA
SIVIL
Casa Cines **C** → **1.7** Café
PINTÍN

Cruce **2.8** →
PonteNov. GOROLFE
Gontán
PASCAIS
LU-P-5707

TEIGUIN
(Teixos)
FURELA
Café **4.6** →
Casa do Franco

SAMOS **S.Salvador**
S.Salvador

Mondaveiga
cristal exposicion ●
Tierra da Luz
Fontearcuda   Labyrinth   Zoó
Montán

A Veiga **H**
Centro **4.2** →

Monasterio

LU-P-5707

Túnel → **S.Martiño**

Alto **3.9** → ▲ 910m   Alto do
Riocabo

Capela
Freituxe
LASTIRES

Renche **1.8** →

SAN XIL

LUSÍO
0.4 **A**   Option Lusío
3.8 S.Cristobo
F
rio Balsa
N.S.de Las
Nieves
Albergue **1.6** → **A** El Beso
A BALSA

LU-633
rio Oribio

2

1

O
puesta
del sol

N

S

salida
del sol
E

Xunta Albergue **0.0** → **1** **A**   **0.7** Opción **0.7**   TRIACASTELA

0.7 km Opción [?] For **route ❶ via San Xil** turn down right> and s/o over main road [!] (*not* left to Samos) onto secondary road and where it veers up left, we turn down right> [**1.0** km] into **A Balsa** [**0.6** km].

1.6 km **A Balsa** (right) ●*Alb.* **Ecologico El Beso** *Priv.[16÷3]* €10 Ⓒ 633 550 558 vegetarian menú *V.* €11. Continue through the hamlet and over river past the tiny chapel to Our Lady of the Snows *ermita N. S. de las Nieves* [**0.5** km] (right) and up steeply on rough woodland path to re-join road at *rest area* [**1.0** km] [☞] with unusual scallop shell motif. We next bypass *San Xil* [**0.6** km] no facilities. From here we have a long climb up by road to our high point today at **alto San Xil** [**1.8** km] (910m). At this point leave the road s/o right down steeply on forest track

3.9 km **Alto San Xil** new woodland path drops down steeply to **Montán** [**1.0** km] with church and cemetery and up through **Fontearcuda** [**1.6** km] where funky 🍵 *Tierra da Luz* welcomes with refreshments by donation. adj. is Samos Labyrinth. Continue over road onto path [*½ km detour to crystals studio Alquimista (António) at Mondaviega]* over a stream back to the road and into *Furela* [**1.8** km]:

4.6 km **Furela** 🍵 *Casa do Franco* café-bar on slip road. Continue to:

1.7 km **Pintín** [☞] •*P¨* **Casa Cines** *x7* €35+ Ⓒ 982 090 837 & 🍵*/bar.* Proceed s/o back over the main road to **Calvor** [**1.4** km] ●*Alb.* **Calvor** *Xunta.[22÷2]* €10 Ⓒ 982 531 266 former school building located on the roadside. Continue over the road through the straggling hamlet of *Hospital* and *Aguiada* [**0.6** km] bar 🍵 *Taberna do Camiño* (currently closed).

2.0 km **Aguiada Hospital** *Centro* (population 36!) site of a former pilgrim hospital where pilgrims who took the **alternative route** via *Samos* join.

For **detour route ❷ via Samos** turn <left at option point in Triacastela down past pilgrim monument and over river to join the busy main road [!]. Use the margins behind the crash barriers wherever possible. Continue alongside the road and cross over to take the access road down to the weir in:

3.8 km **San Cristobo** traditional village on the bank of the river Oribio with its ancient weir and mill buildings. Cross over the river onto a delightful track that winds its way through mixed woodland following the meandering course of the río Oribio to **optional detour** [**0.5** km]

Detour Lusío ●●●● path left for 400m detour to albergue in beautifully restored monastery building in Lusío. ●*Alb.* **Forte de Lusío** *Xunta.[60÷4]* €10 Ⓒ 659 721 324 well restored mansion in this ancient hamlet (the property of Samos monastery). Return to option point to continue s/o along the woodland path before turning <left *(other path continues to Lastires)* over bridge by chapel and up to the main road [**1.2** km] in:

1.8 km **Renche** *Bar* (often closed/ vending machine) continue down (sign Castres) over river and up steeply to *Capela de Freituxe* [**1.5 km**] to take a track back down and over the river again into *San Martiño* [**1.3 km**] chapel and up steeply under main road through **tunnel** [**0.5 km**] over

secondary road onto track above Samos (viewpoint of monastery see photo above) and down steeply past •**Casas de Outeiro** spa €85 © 680 379 969 c/ Fontao and •*P* **Casa da Botica** *x14* €45+ © 982 546 095. ⛲ *A Lareira* by bridge in **Samos town centre** [**1.0 km**]. *(For monastery albergue turn right along the river path and over next bridge).*

4.2 km **Samos** wraps itself around the enormous monastery in this peaceful river valley where time seems to stand still. ❖ *Centre* ⛲ *España* adj. *Alb.* ❶ **Val de Samos** *Priv.*[52÷7] €15 © 609 638 801. Detour right ❷ **Monasterio de Samos** *Conv.*[66÷1] €5 ©982 546 046 Entrance (and key) by petrol pumps. Basic facilities, the simple austerity matches the surroundings. Religious services take place throughout the day with Vespers and pilgrim mass at 19:30 (20:00 Sat / Sun) in the chapel. This is one of the largest and oldest monasteries in the western world founded in VI[th]c on the

asceticism of the Desert Fathers, taking the Benedictine rule in 960. Regular tours take place daily 09:30-18:30 – monastery visit €3. Also ❸ **Externa** *Monasterio* €25 *x15* €25-40 © 643 639 226. The pre Romanesque 'Cypress' chapel *capilla Ciprés S.Salvador IXth* is located to the rear. Legend tells us that to touch the cypress is to remain blister free! Opp. ❹ **Tras do Convento** *Priv.* [6÷1] €12 +2 €25 © 982 546 051. ❖ *From the centre* follow main road out of town (signposted Sarria) passing •*P* **Santa Rosa** *x4* ©633 430 219. •*CR* **Licerio** *x5* €35+ © 982 546 145. •*Hs* **A Veiga** *x15* €40+ © 982 546 052 s/o track by road to picnic site by river and roadside chapel in Tequin *Teixos* [**1.3 km**]. Keep past old route right to Pascais to next turn off right at [**1.5 km**] [**!**].

2.8 km **Cruce** Cross main road by 'new' bridge 🍴 *Pontenova* onto delightful woodland lane up to *iglesia Santa Eulalia* and back down to **Gorolfe** [**2.3 km**] with wayside chapel *San Xumil*. •*H* **Casa de Díaz** *x12* €39+ © 982 547 070 Gorolfe Lugar de Vilachá 4 (900m *off* route). A short stretch of track joins to a quiet country road which we follow over the river (twice) shrine (left) in **Veiga** [**1.6 km**] through **Sivil** with •*P* **A Fonte das Bodas** *x4* €40 ©982 099 103 s/o alongside river through woodland. The road undulates up and down with many turnings but waymarking is reasonable. We next arrive in the hamlet of **Souto de Perros [3.1** km] with wayside chapel *N.S do Camiño* and up through tunnel into **Hospital [0.4** km] where the other route joins at  *Taberna do Camino (currently closed).*

7.4 km **Aguiada Hospital** *Centro* where both routes join.

Continue on dedicated path parallel to the road past ¶ *Pousada Raquel* **S. Mamede del Camino [0.7** km] bypassing hamlets of **San Pedro do Camiño** and **Carballal** to /▲ **Vila de Sarria** €25 © 982 535 467 [**2.2** km] opposite: •*P' **Ana** x6* €30 © 982 531 458 past ¶ *Meson Casa Silva* (menú) to **Vigo de Sarria** (the outskirts of Sarria) [**0.7** km].

3.6 km **Vigo de Sarria.** ❶ *Turismo* © 982 530 099. Albergues ❹-❻ p.54. Follow waymarks to the ancient granite steps *Escalinata Maior* that lead us into the central hub of Sarria:

1.0 km **Sarria** *Centro (rúa Maior)* Albergues ❶ – ⓮. p.54

SARRIA: with its Celtic origins was a major medieval centre for pilgrims with churches, chapels, monasteries and no less than 7 pilgrim hospitals at that time. The ancient atmosphere can still be felt in the attractive old quarter that constitutes the central pilgrim hub of Sarria *rúa Maior*. Now a bustling modern town with a population of 13,500. It has become a major starting point for pilgrims hence the profusion of pilgrim hostels in town providing lodging for budding pilgrims arriving by bus and rail. The advent of the railway in the XIX[th]C saw the town develop eastwards leaving the ancient *camino real* largely intact.

New arrivals are joined by seasoned pilgrims, many arriving by foot from St. Jean Pied de Port in France... or further back (Geneva or Budapest?) The route becomes very busy from this point onwards. If you are just starting out on your pilgrimage note that a few hardened 'veterans' can sometimes begrudge the sudden appearance of new pilgrims on 'their' camino but a smile melts even the most hardened heart and you will generally find welcome and assistance wherever you go. None of us can know the inner motivation or outer circumstances of another. The mark of a pilgrim is an open heart and open mind.

[1]: you now need 2 stamps *sellos* per day to obtain a *Compostela* in Santiago.

[2]: while the following route into Santiago is mapped in 5 stages it can, *and should*, be divided into whatever distances match with your individual level of fitness and desired experience. Towns have a wide range of facilities and consequent higher levels of activity. Villages and isolated hostels offer a quieter and more reflective alternative.

[3]: The Xunta Galicia is constantly re-waymarking different routes into Santiago. This is causing confusion at those points where alternatives are indicated but no information provided as to what each one offers. Few pilgrims take the alternatives which render the distance markers on the ground inaccurate. Route options are described in the text; one reason why a guidebook may be useful.

Historical Monuments: (see the town plan on the following page.) ❶ *Iglesia de Santa Mariña XIX* with its evocative pilgrim mural (*credenciales* issued after pilgrim mass daily at 18:00 (Sun 12:00). At the top of rúa Maior ❷ *Iglesia del Salvador XIII* with its tympanum of Christ in Majesty and the Tree of Life (mass Sun 18:00). Opp: ❸ *Hospital de San Anton XVI antiguo hospital de peregrino* (now courts of Justice). ❹ *Fortaleza de Sarria y Torres XIII* castle (ruins). The camino continues to ❺ *Monasterio (Mosteiro) de la Magdalena (Convento de la Merced) XIII* with fine plateresque façade and now an albergue that issues *credenciales. Daily mass at 20:00 (Sun 13:00).* Note all times liable to change. The camino continues down to the medieval bridge **Ponte Áspera** *(Rough Bridge)* over the río Celerio.

Personal Reflections:

VIGO DE SARRIA ❶ *Turismo* © 982 530 099 (outskirts) *Albergues* av. price €12+ **Ⓐ** A Pedra *Priv.*[23÷5]+4* © 982 530 130. Opp. **Ⓑ** Oasis *Priv.[27÷4]* © 605 948 644 adj. •*P* Siete *x6* €35+ © 982 044 208. S/o into busy Calvo Sotelo ⚄/•*Hs* Cristal *x15* €45 © 669 799 512. ⚄/**Ⓒ** Barullo *Priv.[20÷1]+2* ©982 876 357 Praza de Galicia, 40 and **Ⓓ** Credencial *Priv.[28÷2]* © 982 876 455 Rúa do Peregrino, 50-bajo. Just off route on Calvo Sotelo is **Ⓔ**Alma do Camiño *Priv.[100÷10]* © 982 876 768 and further along on c/ Ameneirizas •*P*Blasones *x14* €20-40 © 652 256 226. •*P* Rúa Peregrino *x11* €50 © 982 886 662. •*H*```` Alfonso IX *x60* €60+ © 982 530 005 and **Ⓕ** Puente Ribeira *Priv.[28÷3]+8* © 982 876 789 Rúa do Peregrino, Nº 23 - Bajo. •*H*``` Oca Villa €45 © 982 533 873 (left 100m) c/ Benigno Quiroga. •*P* O Camiño *x3* €35+ © 626 205 172.

SARRIA CENTRO *Albergues* **❶** – **⓮** av. price €12: **❶** Casa Peltre *Priv [22÷3]* © 606 226 067. •*P*Escalinata *x8* €40 © 982 530 259. **❨** Rúa Maior Nº64 **❷** Mayor *Priv.[16÷3]* © 685 148 474. Nº79 **❸** Xunta *[40÷1]* © 660 396 813 (€10). Nº62 •*P*``` Aqua *x3* €45 © 620 988 251. Nº44 **❹** O Durmiñento *Priv.[38÷5]+1* © 982 531 099 roof terrace. Nº53 •*P*```Casa Barán *x4* €75 © 982 876 487. Nº57 **❺** Internacional *Priv.[38÷4]+2* © 982 535 109 roof terrace. Nº49 **❻** Obradoiro *Priv.[38÷2]* © 982 532 442 garden terrace. Nº31 **❼** Los Blasones *Priv.*[42÷4]* © 600 512 565 rear patio. Nº29 **❽** El Bordón *Priv.[6÷4]* +4 © 982 530 652. Nº19 •*P* Mesón Camino Francés © 982 532 351 (opp. Mesón O Tapas). Nº10 **❾** Don Álvaro *Priv.[40÷6]+7* © 982 531 592 rear patio. Nº4 **❿** Matías *Priv.[30÷1]+6* © 982 534 285 adj. ⑆ *Matias Locanda Italiana*. •*H*``Nova *x17* €40+ © 982 605 021, pl. Constitución, 4. **⓫** Sleeping Sarria *Priv.* 16 beds in shared rooms of up to 4 people © 689 319 941 c/Esqueirodos,1. **⓬** Monasterio de la Magdalena *Priv.[110÷5]* Av. de la Merced, © 982 533 568 'twinned' with albergue Seminario Menor in Santiago. **⓭** San Lázaro *Priv.[27÷3]+4* © 982 530 626 c/San Lázaro,7. •*P* La Casona de Sarria *x6* €50 © 982 535 556 Rúa San Lázaro 24. **⓮** Andaina *Priv.[26÷2]* © 628 232 103 Rúa Calvo Sotelo, 11.•*P*` La Estación *x5* €30 © 658 094 994 c/ Matías López,106. •*P*Matias Rooms *x10* €35+ Calle Rosalia de Castro, 19 (same ownership as albergue Matias © 982 534 285). In the 'new' town •*P*` Casa Matías *x10* €26 © 659 160 498 Calvo Sotelo,39. •*H*` Mar de Plata *x25* €50+ © 982 530 724. Adj. railway station •*Hr*` Roma © 982 532 211 Calvo Sotelo,2.

Restaurants: (see map) Variety of lively riverside cafes on the *Malecon*. Pilgrims tend to congregate around rúa Maior: at Nº29 ⑆ *Anduriñas* vegetarian options, also Nº4 ⑆ *Matias Locanda Italiana* or 'hidden' gem ⑆ *A Travesía Dos Soños* with rear terrace 'tucked behind' the church on Travesia Iglesia. For tranquil setting on the river ⑆ *O Chanto* & ⑆ *Casa del Barrio*.
Pilgrim equipment: •*Peregrinoteca* c/ Benigno Quiroga, 16 (08:00–20:00) © 982 530 190 popular 'Aladdin's Cave' of equipment for pilgrims (see photo previous page). •*Xesta* c/José Sánachez Arias •*Kilometr 112* rua do Peregrino,37. ❒ *Lavandería Aclareo* r/Matías López.

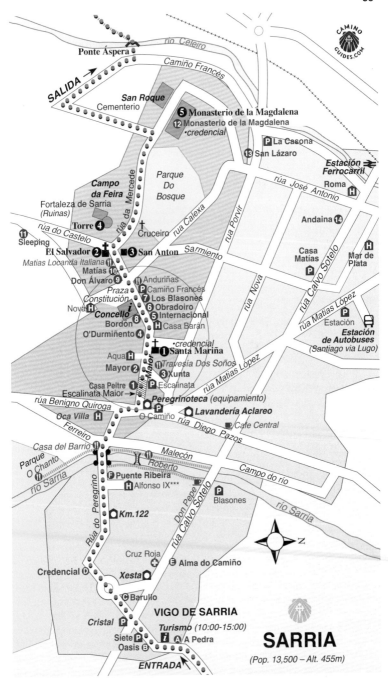

03 SARRIA – PORTOMARÍN
Santiago – 117.4 km (*72.9 ml*)

....	--- ---	11.4	--- ---	50%
	--- ---	10.7	--- ---	48%
	--- ---	0.6	--- ---	2%
Total km		**22.7 km** (*14.1 ml*)		

Total ascent **940m** ±*1½ hr*

Alto.m ▲ Alto Momientos **660m** (*2,165 ft*)

< Ⓐ Ⓗ > ➋ Barbadelo (❶ **3.7 km** - ❺ **4.5km**) ➋ Morgade **12.4 km**.
➋ Ferreiros **13.8** ➋ Mercadoiro **17.3** ➋ Vilacha **20.4 km**.

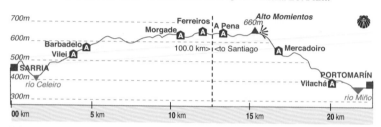

The Practical Path: The majority of today's stage is on lovely woodland paths and gravel tracks. Apart from the bare flanks around the high point on the Peña do Cervo at Momientos (above Portomarín) much of the remainder is along forest paths and tree-lined lanes. So we have good shade from the sun or shelter from the driving rain. We will pass through many small hamlets that seem to blend seamlessly one into the next. Several new cafés offer refreshment stops along the way.

The Mystical Path: *To err is human, to forgive, divine.* Alexander Pope. We cannot live in the past and we try in vain to live with the idea of some future golden age. The only place we can truly inhabit is the present. The rest is fantasy; some painful some pleasurable.

Personal Reflections: *"... I reflect on the extraordinary revelation of the third secret of Fátima. We are all fallen angels struggling to find our wings so that we can fly back home to the Divine. If God is my Father what does that make me and, by extension, all my fellow brothers and sisters? We each share the same Identity and the same Inheritance. And so I come full circle, back to the place where I began and to the realisation that the only way out... is in. External authority is flawed and must collapse. The Voice for God is within and urges each one of us, as children of one God, to become the authors of own awakening..."*

0.0 km **Sarria** *Centro* from albergue ❶ in Sarria head up c/Mayor past the church of Santa Mariña with its sombre medieval pilgrim murals and past the town hall (left) *Casa do Concello*. Next we pass the intimate *Praza da Constitución* with albergues, cafes and restaurants and towards the top of

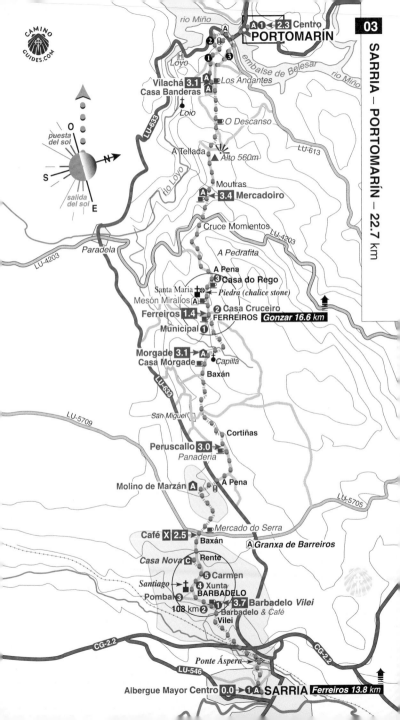

rio Miño

A1 ◄ **2.3** Centro
PORTOMARÍN

embalse de Belesar

rio Miño

2
A
1
3

H
Loyo

Vilachá **3.1** ►
Casa Banderas **A**

Los Andantes

Loio

O Descanso

A Tellada
Alto 560m

LU-533

rio Loyo

LU-613

Moutras
A ◄ **3.4** Mercadoiro

Cruce Momientos

LU-4203

A Pedrafita

Paradela

LU-4203

A Pena
3 Casa do Rego
Piedra (chalice stone)

Santa Maria
Mesón Mirallos **A**
Ferreiros **1.4** ►

2 Casa Cruceiro
FERREIROS *Gonzar 16.6 km*

Municipal **1**

Morgade **3.1** ►
Casa Morgade **A**
Capilla

Baxán

LU-633

San Miguel

Cortiñas

Peruscallo **3.0** ►
Panadería

Molino de Marzán **A**
A Pena

LU-5709

LU-5705

Mercado do Serra

Café **X** **2.5** ►
Baxán
A *Granxa de Barreiros*

Casa Nova **C**
Rente

5 Carmen
Santiago →
4 Xunta
BARBADELO
Pombal **3**
108 km **2** **1** **3.7** ► Barbadelo *Vilei*
Barbadelo & Café
Vilei

CG-2.2
CG-2.2

Ponte Áspera →

LU-546

Albergue Mayor Centro **0.0** ► **1** **A** **SARRIA** *Ferreiros 13.8 km*

the street (left) Church of St. Saviour *Igrexa de San Salvador XIIIthc* with its primitive Romanesque tympanum over the main door. St. Anthony's pilgrim Hospice stood opposite (now courts of Justice). Here we turn right> to pass the ruins of the Sarria castle *Fortaleza de Sarria* (left) only one of

the 4 original towers remains. The castle was destroyed during the uprising of the peasantry against the aristocracy in the XVthc known as the *Irmandiños*. We pass a stone *cruceiro* (right) with views back over the town and up past the country market *Campo da Feira* (left) which has existed here since the XIVthc and down to the plateresque façade of the **Mosteiro da Madalena** [0.7 km] (also provides *credencial*) originally instituted in the XIIIthc, later coming under the Augustinian rule. We finally head down past the cemetery and *Capela de San Lázaro* to cross the road and río Celeiro over the medieval 'Rough Bridge' **Ponte Áspera** [0.5 km] due to its coarsely cut stone. A path now winds between river and railway before crossing the line in *Santi Michaelis* under road viaduct to cross a stream and climb up through delightful ancient woodland to join the road in **Vilei** an extension of **Barbadelo** [2.5 km].

3.7 km Barbadelo *Vilei* 🪧/*Alb.*
❶ Casa Barbadelo *Priv.[48÷6]*
€12 +*11* €50 © 982 531 934 *www.barbadelo.com* garden + swimpool.
❷ 108 km *Priv.[14÷5]+* €8-15 ©
634 894 524. ❸ O Pombal *Priv.[12÷1]* €12 © 686 718 732. 200m off route below *Igrexa de Santiago XIIthc*
Romanesque with a fine tympanum

and statue of St. James. Pilgrim mass 19:00 (check notice board). *[The area is known locally as Mosteiro in reference to a monastery founded here as early as the IXthc].* ❹ Barbadelo *Xunta.[18÷2]* €10 © 660 396 814, former school on **village green** [0.7 km]. Behind the albergue is a summer cantina and at the top of the lane (200m off route) ❺ Casa de Carmen *Priv.***[24÷3]* €11 + €35 © 982 532 294 in restored XVIIthc farmhouse with terrace and private chapel *Capela de San Silvestre*. Continue to **Rente** [1.0 km] s/o along woodland paths through ancient oak and chestnut groves and cross main road [0.7 km]:

2.5 km Cruce 🪧*Mercado Serra.* S/o past [🚻] to ●*Alb.* **Molino de Marzán** *Priv.[14÷1]* €12 © 679 438 077. Cross road into **A Pena** and **Peruscallo.**

3.0 km Peruscallo 🪧 *Panaderia Peruscallo.* S/o through **Cortiñas**, **Casal** and into **A Brea** [2.1 km] passing ('old' km 99,5 now 101,996) into:

3.1 km Morgade ●*Alb.* **Casa Morgade** *Priv.[6÷1]* €14 +*13* €40 © 982

531 250 with popular café. Pass stone chapel and continue on track down (through!) the Ferreiros stream. This is rural Galicia at her best; green and often wet underfoot with the earthy smell of cow dung. Narrow laneways with granite stepping-stones raised above flood levels provide a gentle climb up to:

1.4 km Ferreiros With the modern ⊪/*Alb.*❶ **Casa Cruceiro** *Priv.[24÷2]* €12 +2 €50 - €70 ©982 541 240 <u>www.casacruceirodeferreiros.com</u>. *(New 'official' waymark 100.746 km makes this the last chance for a compostela!)* Just below (left) is ❷ **Ferreiros** *Xunta. [22÷1]* €10 © 982 157 496 former

schoolhouse. S/o past **Mirallos [0.3 km]** 🍴 *Mesón Mirallos* © 982 157 162 (+ 12 bunks €-donativo 'unofficial').

50m (left) beyond Iglesia Santa María is the ancient ⚜ *Chalice Stone*. S/o to tranquil hamlet of **A Pena [0.4 km]**. Up steeply to **As Rozas [0.8 km]** [🛏] and the high point *Pena dos Corvos 660m* at Cruce Momientos [1.3 km] with fine views over the reservoir as we begin our descent into the río Miño valley and **Mercadoiro [0.7 km]**:

3.4 km Mercadoiro A delightful hamlet with an official population of – one! ●*Alb.* **Mercadoiro** *Priv. [22÷3]*€12 +4 €45 © 982 545 359. With popular ⊪/🍴 *Bodeguiña* (pilgrim menu). Continue through **Moutras** and **A Parrocha**. *[off route left is the remote valley of Loio with the ruins of the Monastery of Santa María de Loio –*

birthplace of the Order of Santiago in the XII[th]c]. Shortly after we reach the high point we pass 🍴 *O Descanso* with fine views over the Minho valley into:

3.1 km Vilachá ●*Alb.* **Casa Banderas** *[9÷1]* €13 (€27 media pensión) *+1* €40 © 682 179 589 and ●*Alb.* **Vilachá** *[10÷1]* €13 © 696 004 491. 🍴*Casa Susana* rest area/snacks. ⊪ *Los Andantes V.* popular pizzería. Continue s/o to option **[0.6 km]**. The route descends *very* steeply to the bridge spanning the Miño basin.

Option ❶ Original route (fading waymarks) s/o at crossroads and first left along country lane onto the quieter LU-613. For new routes turn down left **[0.4 km]**. Note both the next 2 options exit abruptly onto the busy LU-633 *[!]*. ❷ S/o for the short but steep and rough descent on narrow gorge (slippy when wet). ❸ Turn left and then first right for the longer (+0.4 km) but less steep route. Both end up directly on the main road opp. *Alb.* **A Fontana de Luxo** © 645 649 496. *[left +1.9 km ▪H Meson do Loyo x9 €40+ © 982 545 012]*. Turn right and cross bridge to **roundabout [0.6 km]** at **Portomarín:**

[To continue direct to Gonzar & Santiago follow the road to the left over the bridge (200m) see map below]. To visit or stay in Portomarín take the steep staircase in front, part of the original medieval bridge across the river Miño. The arch and *capela de Santa María de las Nieves*, along with several other historic monuments, were all removed to the high ground around Portomarín when the dam was built to create the Belesar reservoir in 1962. Climb the stairs for the first (lower) of 16 albergues [**0.1** km] with fine views over the river and reservoir.

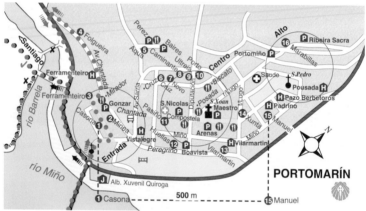

2.3 km **Portomarín** ◖*Albergues Entrada: Alb.* ❶Casona de Ponte *Priv.[47÷5]* €12 *+16* €50+ ☎ 982 169 862 *www.casonadaponte.com* c/ Capela. ❷**Pons Minea** *Priv.[24÷3]* *+6* €40+ ☎ 610 737 995 Av. Sarria. ❸**Ferramenteiro** *Priv.*[130÷1]* €12 ☎ 982 545 362 c/Chantada. ❹**Folgueira** *Priv.[32÷1]* €12 ☎ 982 545 166 down Av. Chantada (exit). ◖**Other Lodging** *Entrada:* popular ▮*O Mirador (see Hostal El Padrino)* •*P* **Gonzar** *[12÷1]* €12 *x6* €30+ ☎ 982 545 275 + bar. •*H*****Ferramenteiro** *x22* €55-80 ☎ 982 545 361. •*Spa H*****Vistalegre** *x20* €80+ ☎ 982 545 076 *c/ Compostela* N°29 &@N°10 •*P*****Casa S. Nicolas** *x12* €55+ ☎ 669 497 243 *www.casasannicolas.es.*

Continue up the cobbled main street Av. Compostela with its stone colonnades and various shops / cafés leading to the lively central square *Praza Conde de Fenosa* with choice of restaurants, bars and lodging and the *Casa do Concello* & ❶ *Turismo* 14:00–20:00 *Summer*. Overlooking all this is the austere Romanesque fortress church of St. John with links to the Knights of Saint John *Igrexa de San Juan / San Xoán* (also San Nicholas!). It was rebuilt from its original site now submerged under the waters of the Belesar reservoir and ascribed to the workshop of Master Mateo who carved the Pórtico da Gloria in Santiago. Built as both a place of worship and defence, with its 4 defensive towers and battlements (crenellated parapet). The church has a single barrel vaulted nave and semicircular apse and prominent rose window. Daily mass at 20:00 (Sundays 12:30) times may vary. Parque Antonio Sanz with Church of St. Peter *Iglesia San Pedro* with Romanesque doorway.

❨*Albergues Centro:* ❺Aqua *Priv.[10÷1]* €12 +3 €35+ ⓒ 608 921 372 c/ Barreiros. ❻Casa Cruz *Priv.[16÷1]* €12 ⓒ 982 545 140 *c/Benigno Quiroga* Nº16 &@ Nº12 ❼Novo Porto *Priv.[22÷1]* €12 ⓒ 982 545 277. ❽El Caminante *Priv.[12÷4]* €12 +15 €30+ ⓒ 982 545 176 c/Sánchez Carro, 7. ❾Ultreia *Priv.**[14÷1] +5 €35+ ⓒ 982 545 067 *c/Diputación* Nº9 opp. Nº8 ❿Porto Santiago *Priv.**[7÷1]€15 +5 €40+ ⓒ 618 826 515. ⓫Pasiño a Pasiño *Priv.[30÷6]* €12 ⓒ 665 667 243 r/Compostela 25. ⓬Huellas *Priv.[6÷1]* €12 +3 €35+ ⓒ 681 398 278 *www.alberg*u*ehuellas.com* *r/ Peregrino* Nº15 &@Nº11 ⓭Villamartín *Priv.[22÷2]* €12 ⓒ 982 545 054. ⓮Portomarín *Xunta.[86÷6]* €10 ⓒ 660 396 816 original hostel renovated with all mod cons. ⓯ Manuel *Priv.[16÷2]* €12 +4 €25 ⓒ 982 545 385 c/ Miño 1. ❨*Other Lodging Centro: Praza Conde Fenosa* with lively bars & restaurants •*P*ˮArenas ⓒ 982 545 386. •*H*ˮ Villajardín *x36* €40-70 ⓒ 982 545 054 *www.hotelvillajardin.com* r/Miño 14. •*P*ˮˮCasa do Maestro *x10* €50-70 ⓒ 626 510 806 *www.casadomaestro.com* adj. S.Xoan on *r/Fraga Iribarne* Nº1 &@ Nº5 •*P*ˈ Mar *x8* €34-40 ⓒ 622 611 211 &@ Nº18 •*Hs*ˮˮEl Padrino *x6* €60-70 ⓒ 982 545 323. •*H*ˮPazo de Berbetoros *Marquesa x3* €60+ ⓒ 982 545 292 r/San Pedro. •*P* Pérez *x10* €35+ ⓒ 982 545 040 Pl. A. Española. •*P* Baires *[5÷1]* €15 +3 €30+ ⓒ 645 118 958.

❨*Albergue Alto:* ⓰ Casa do Marabillas *Priv.[16÷4]* €14 +2 €30+ ⓒ 982 189 086 Camiño do Monte 3.❨*Other Lodging Alto* •*P*ˈ Portomiño *x24* €35+ ⓒ 982 547 575 *www.portomino.com* c/Sánchez Carro, 23 *(see Rst. Portomiño)*. •*P* Ribeira Sacra *x4* €30-50 ⓒ 608 921 372 Camiño do Monte. •*P*ˮˮPosada *x34* €55-77 ⓒ 982 545 200. *[Next albergue: Gonzar – 7.7 km].*

Personal Reflections:

04 PORTOMARÍN – PALAS DE REI
Santiago – 94.7 km (*58.8 ml*)

▥▥▥▥▥	--- ---	19.8 --- ---	80%
▬▬▬▬	--- ---	4.8 --- ---	20%
▬▬▬	--- ---	0.0	
Total km		**24.6** km (*15.3 ml*)	

▲ Total Ascent **1,050**m ±*1¾ hr*
Alto.m ▲ Sierra Ligonde **720**m (*2,362 ft*)
< ▲ ▥ > ➔ Gonzar **7.7** km ➔ Hospital **11.0** ➔ Ventas de Narón **12.6** km
➔ Ligonde **16.3** km ➔ Eirexe **16.9** ➔ Portos **19.1** ➔ Os Chacotes **23.4** km

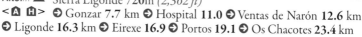

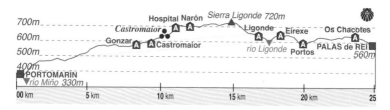

The Practical Path: A day of varied terrain as we start by climbing up a peaceful woodland path on the recommended camino *complementario* (the 'official' route via S. Roque is 0.7 km longer and all by road). Both routes join on the main road LU-633 which we have to cross on several occasions [!] before leaving it to climb around *Castromaior* (well worth the short detour) and the *Sierra Ligonde* descending to Portos which offers us the detour to Vilar de Donas. Then comes a gentler climb around the side of Rosary Heights *Alto Rosario* to drop down finally to Palas de Rei. Prepare for an early start if you intend to take the longer detour to Vilar de Donas.

The Mystical Path: *The foolish man seeks happiness in the distance; The wise man grows it under his feet. J R Oppenheimer.* Will you make time to detour to this mystical resting place of the Knights of Saint James? Here effigies of the knights in their armour are watched over by the beautiful frescoes that adorn the walls of this sacred temple dedicated to Saint Saviour. A pilgrim must travel on two paths simultaneously. The tourist will look for the stone altar – the pilgrim an altered state. The one seeks sacred sites – the other *in-sight*. Will you make time today to detour into the inner mystery?

Personal Reflections: *"... The incessant rain pounds down as heavy as when it started a week ago. The country is awash; roads have turned to rivers. I sat for a while at the base of the ancient oak and felt its solid support. I don't know how long I had been in this altered state, induced as much by physical exhaustion as any ecstatic revelation. And I don't know how long they had been there but they helped me to my feet; 3 pilgrims from 3 different countries but part of one family.*

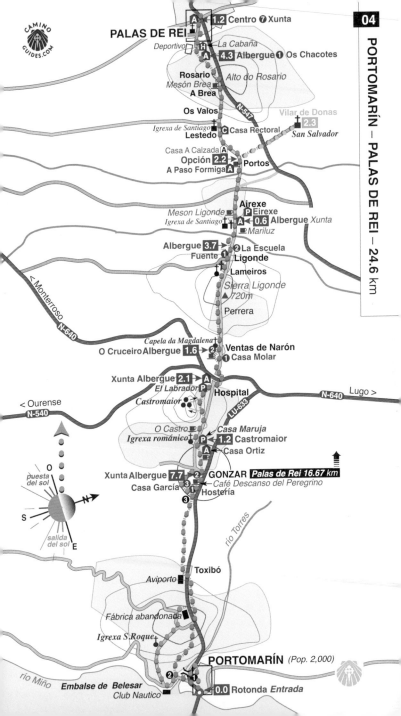

CAMINO GUIDES.COM

PALAS DE REI

A ← 1.2 Centro ❼ Xunta

H *La Cabaña*
Deportivo
A ← 4.3 Albergue ❶ Os Chacotes

Rosario *Alto do Rosario*
Mesón Brea ■
A Brea

Os Valos
Igrexa de Santiago † C Casa Rectoral
Lestedo

Vilar de Donas
2.3
San Salvador

N-547

Casa A Calzada A
Opción 2.2 →
A Paso Formiga A ← **Portos**

Meson Ligonde P **Airexe** Eirexe
Igrexa de Santiago † A ← 0.6 Albergue *Xunta*
P *Mariluz*

Albergue 3.7 → ❷ **La Escuela**
Fuente ❶ **Ligonde**
† **Lameiros**

Sierra Ligonde
▲ *720m*

Perrera

Capela da Magdalena †
O Cruceiro **Albergue** 1.6 → ❷ **Ventas de Narón**
❶ **Casa Molar**

Xunta Albergue 2.1 → A
El Labrador P
Castromaior **Hospital**

LU-633

N-640 Lugo >

< Ourense
N-540

O *Castro* ■ *Casa Maruja*
Igrexa románico † P 1.2 **Castromaior**
A ← *Casa Ortiz*

O
puesta del sol
S
N
E
salida del sol

Xunta Albergue 7.7 → ❷ **GONZAR** *Palas de Rei 16.67 km*
Casa García ❸ ← *Café Descanso del Peregrino*
❶ **Hostería**
❸

rio Torres

Toxibó
Aviporto

Fábrica abandonada ■

Igrexa S.Roque †

PORTOMARÍN *(Pop. 2,000)*

rio Miño
Embalse de Belesar
Club Nautico ■
❷
❶
0.0 **Rotonda** *Entrada*

0.0 km **Portomarín** from albergue❶
Option ❶ make your way back down
to the main road at roundabout *or* via
Av. Chantada and take the bridge over
the río Torres [**0.4 km**]. *Option* ❷:
*Turn <left for the longer 'official' road
route via Club Nautico and San Roque* or right> for the peaceful woodland
path to join the pilgrim track by the main road. Cross over by the abandoned
Fábrica (alt. route joins from the left) and re-cross by Aviporto fertilizer plant
in **Toxibó**. Continue past woodland picnic site [☕] and *option* ❸: <left for
alt. track to Gonzar or continue alongside the main road (same distance) past
the first of three albergues ❶ **Hostería** *Priv.[20÷2]* €12 +*13* €40+ ☏ 982
154 878 *www.hosteriadegonzar.com*

7.7 km Gonzar 🍴 *Descanso Peregrino* the first in nearly 8 km so often busy.
It adjoins *Alb.* ❷ **Gonzar** *Xunta.[28÷1]* €10 ☏ 982 157 840 also directly on
main road. Around the corner (100m) *Alb.* ❸ **Casa Garcia** *Priv.[26÷2]* €10
+*4* €35 ☏ 982 157 842 with covered courtyard in quiet location off main
road with 🍴. Continue along main road and turn off <left onto track past
the new 🍴/●*Alb.* **Ortiz** *Priv.[12÷1]* €12 +*4* €40 ☏ 982 099 416.

1.2 km **Castromaior** church of
Santa María. •*P˙* **Casa Maruja** *x4*
€16+ ☏ 982 189 054. •*P˙* **Perdigueira**
x4 €40+ ☏ 690 852 026. Continue
up steeply past 🍴 *O Castro*. **Detour:**
(150m): *to the ancient Castro
inhabited from the IV[th]c BCE to the start
of the Roman occupation. With 360°
views of the surrounding countryside.*
Continue through woodland into:

2.1 km **Hospital de la Cruz** where the N-540 cuts through this ancient
village (medieval pilgrim hospice no longer visible) but hospitality awaits at
•*Hs* **El Labrador** *x9* €35+ ☏ 982 545 303 & 🍴. ●*Alb.* **Hospital de la Cruz**
Xunta [32÷2] €10 another conversion of a school building by the main road
(N-540 Ourense – Lugo) take the minor road flyover to the next village:

1.6 km **Ventas de Narón** *Alb.* ❶ **Casa Molar** *Priv.[18÷2]* €10 +*2* €30 ☏
696 794 507 🍴. *Alb.* ❷ **O Cruceiro** *Priv.**[26÷3]* €12 +*6* €30 ☏ 658 064
917 also with popular 🍴/🍴. Romanesque **Capela da Magdalena** former
hospital of the Knights Templar whose emblematic stamp is available from
the custodian. *[The area was scene of a fierce battle in 840 between Moor and
Christian but there is nothing here now to disturb the peace beyond pilgrim
chatter in the cafés].* We climb the Sierra Ligonde to the high point (720m)
passing dog kennels *perreras Alejo* before dropping down to the hamlet of

Lameiros with the *Antiguo Hospital de Peregrinos* (now a private house) and the *Casa da Carneiro* which provided hospitality to the Roman emperor Charles V and also King Philip of Spain while on his way to marry Mary Tudor. Continue on country road passing XVII[th]c wayside cross (left) by gnarled oak tree.

3.7 km **Ligonde** equally ancient and long associated with the camino with its *Cementerio de Peregrinos*. •CR **Tania** x3 €60-120 Ⓒ 604 047 316. *Alb.* ❶ **Fuente del Peregrino** *Asoc.[9÷2]* €-donativo Ⓒ 687 550 527 voluntary hospitaleros of Christian group Agape. ❷ **Escuela de Ligonde** *Muni.* *[20÷1]* €10 Ⓒ 982 153 483. Igrexa de Santiago has a Romanesque porch. Opposite the Albergue is a short track down over the río Ligonde passing ⁛/≜ *Casa Mari Luz* (right) up past cruceiro Igrexa Santiago into:

0.6 km **Airexe** ●*Alb.* **Airexe** *Xunta.[20÷1]* €10 former school building at crossroads with all facilities. To the rear is •P **Eirexe** x5 €25-50 Ⓒ 982 153 475 with bar-menú. At the crossroads is ⁛*Meson Ligonde*. Continue on quiet country road passing diminutive Iglesia de Santiago de Ligonde and roadside cross. We now climb gently to a crossing of 5 roads with open views of the surrounding countryside before dropping down into **Portos** ●*Alb.* **A Paso de Formiga** (Ants Way!) *Priv.[12÷2]* €13 +2 €50 Ⓒ 618 984 605 *www. apasodeformiga.com*. Continue s/o to:

2.2 km **Opción** *Detour* **Portos** *A Calzada* With closed *Alb.& café* **A Calzada** and picnic area.

Detour: 4.6 km ● ● ● ● **Vilar de Donas**. (return the same way). National monument and ancient seat of the Knights of Santiago. Closed Mondays and holidays (check in Portos for opening times). The Church of El Salvador is primarily XIV[th]c but its origins go back to the formation of a nunnery here in the X[th]c (hence the appellation Donas). The stone effigies of the knights and its unique frescoes are hauntingly expressive. *Directions:* Turn right off the camino (opposite A Calzada) along quiet country lane across the main road [1.1 km] (N-547 Palas de Rei – Lugo) passing rest area *área de descanso* (right) for remaining [1.2 km] to:

2.3 km **Vilar de Donas – Igrexa San Salvador.**

From *A Calzada* continue along pathways into and through the hamlet of **Lestedo** [**0.6** km] ⛩/•*CR*. **Rectoral de Lestedo** *x7* €80+ ⓒ 982 153 435 converted from original pilgrim hospital & priests house *casa rectoral*. We pass Iglesia Santiago De Lestedo and cemetery and then **Os Valos** into *A Brea* [**1.8** km] ⛩ *Mesón A Brea* on the main N-547. A short woodland path at the back of the restaurant takes us up to **Alto Rosario** [**0.9** km]. *[Here, before the trees were planted, you could see the sacred peak above Santiago Pico Sacro and on entering the hamlet of Rosario pilgrims would start to recite the Rosary, hence the name].* We now pass through the hamlet which adjoins the main road before entering the suburbs of Palas de Rei and its delightful municipal parkland [**1.0** km] *Área recreativa de Os Chacotes*.

4.3 km Palas de Rei *Os Chacotes* *Alb.*
❶ **Os Chacotes** *Xunta.[112÷3]* €8 ⓒ
607 481 536 peaceful parkland setting.
•*H*‴**Complejo La Cabana** *x30* €45-59
ⓒ 982 380 750. Keep s/o past sports hall
into town ❖ **Entrada** c/Paz (left 50m).
Note: private albergues av. price €10-15. ❷**Mesón de Benito** *Priv.[78÷6]*
ⓒ 982 103 386 +300m. ❸**Zendoira**

Priv.[50÷2] +6 €30+ ⓒ 629727605 Amado Losada 10 (off Av.Ourense).
❖ Continue into town on *rua Cruceiro* past •*Hs* **O Castelo** *x8* €45+ ⓒ
618 401 130. ⛩/•*P* **O Cruceiro** *x10* €45+ ⓒ 649 629 725. •*Hs* **Mica** *x16*
€50+ ⓒ 689 339 770 and •*P* **Casa Curro** *x8* €40 (1). Up right on *c/ Outeiro*
❹**Outeiro** *Priv.[60÷8]* ⓒ 982 380 242 adj. Plaza de Galicia.

❖ At ⛩ *O Cruceiro* take the lane s/o (left) past parish church of **San Tirso** open daily with mass at 19:00 *[built in the XI*[th]*C but now only retaining its original Romanesque doorway].* [⛩]. Down steps to main road by modern ❺**San Marcos** *Priv.[60÷10]+20* €55+ⓒ 982 380 711 *www.alberguesanmarcos.es* Cross road to ⛩/ *Alb.* ❻ **Castro** *Priv.***[60÷9]* ⓒ 609 080 655 on corner. ◆ Sign up right for •*Hr*‴**Benilde** *x7* ⓒ 982 380 717 *www.hotelcasabenilde.com* on r/Mercado opp. •*P* **Pardellas** ⓒ 982 380 181. ◆ Take steps down into r/ Iglesia past popular ⛩ *Forxa* with rear patio *(left).*

1.2 km Palas de Rei *Centro* ❼ Xunta *[60÷5]* €10 original hostel popular owing to its central location *Av. Compostela* Nº**19,** directly opp. Town Hall *Casa Concello.* ❖ *up (right)* @Nº**24** •*P* **Fonte** *x10* €50 ⓒ 671 231 991 *www.pensionafonte.com* @Nº**16** ❽*Alb/P*‴**Arenas Palas** *Priv.[24÷4]* €4 +15 €35-50 ⓒ 982 380 326 +*250m* •*P* **Cabalo Verde** *x25* €25-50 ⓒ 679 911 186 Trv/Feira +*500m* •*P* **Palas** *x15* €40+ ⓒ 982 380 065 c/S.Tirso. ❖ *down (left)* @Nº**21** ⛩ *bar*/•*P* **Plaza** *x14* €25-45 ⓒ 660 875 921 adj. ⛩ *A Nova Terra pulperia* ❖ By Concello **Travesía del Peregrino**. @Nº**10** •*P* **Casa Camiño** *x15* €40-55 ⓒ 982 374 066 (+ **Casa Camiño II** @Nº**8** same ownership) to the rear on r/Hortas •*P*‴**As Hortas** *x7* €59-79 ⓒ 626 518 388 with quiet garden *www.pensionashortas.com*

PALAS de REI

❾ BuenCamino *Priv.*[42÷8]* ⓒ 982 380 233. At exit of town *+300m*:
❿ A Casiña di Marcello *Priv.[16÷2]* ⓒ 640 723 903 c/Camiño de abaixo.
+1km •*Hs* **Ponterroxán** *x18* €25-30 ⓒ 982 380 132. *[Next albergue: Mato Casanova – 6.3 km].*

Up town services (see town plan): ☐ *lavandería do Camiño* + *Fisioterapia Ricardo Velho* ⓒ 601 624 724 🛒 **Eroski**.

Palas de Rei ❶ *Turismo* *Casa Concello* Av. de Compostela 28 ⓒ 982 380 001. Note the regular Lugo – Santiago bus stops here. This busy town straddles the camino and was a 'compulsory' stop in the *Codex Calixtinus*. Little remains to remind us of its illustrious past but the name derives from *Pallatium Regis* palace of the Visigothic king Witiza who reigned from 702 – 710. The Church of ***Santiago de Alba*** *XII[th]c* has a Romanesque portal and scallop shell motifs are visible in the town. Today, it is an administrative centre with good modern facilities serving a population of 3,600 mostly engaged in the dairy industry and the well known Ulloa cheese.

Personal Reflections:

05 PALAS DE REI – RIBADISO (ARZÚA)
Santiago – 70.1 km (*43.6 ml*)

....	--- ---	18.9 --- ---	72%
————	--- ---	6.6 --- ---	25%
————	--- ---	0.8 --- ---	3%
Total km		**26.3** km (*16.3 ml*)	

Total ascent **820m** ±1¼ hr
Alto.m ▲ O Coto **515m** (*1,670 ft*)
< Ⓐ Ⓗ > ⊃ San Xulián **3.6** km ⊃ Casanova **5.9** km ⊃ O Coto **8.7** km
⊃ Melide **15.1** km ⊃ Boente **21.0** km ⊃ Castañeda **23.2** km.

The Practical Path: Today we cross 6 shallow river valleys and ¾ on pathways mostly through delightful woodland that helps to stifle the noise from the busy N-547 which we cross and re-cross all the way to Arzúa (29.5 km). This busy town is where the northern route *camino del norte* joins the *camino francés* and the route gets ever busier as we approach Santiago. Melide (15.1 km) makes a good halfway stop where we can sample the renowned octopus *pulpo Gallega* and explore the historic old town. Melide is also where pilgrims walking the original way *camino primitivo* via Oviedo join the burgeoning band of seekers. Ribadiso de Baixo on the Río Iso makes a peaceful end point before the relative busyness of the final stages.

The Mystical Path: *Walking, I am listening to a deeper way... all my ancestors are behind me. 'Be still, they say. Watch and listen. You are the result of the love of thousands'. Linda Hogan.* Will you see the figure of Santiago in the flyover? Why do we follow his way? He has many names, but who was he really and what significance does he play in our story?

Personal Journal: *"... In each moment I sense my guides setting up situations for me to learn the next lesson. I have an image of angels urging me to learn through grace rather than grit. So my angelic escort set me up Toshio, just when I had lost my inner way and was confused as to my motivation. And he asks me three questions: each one a reminder of my reason for doing this pilgrimage and an invaluable aid to its accomplishment.*

0.0 km **Palas de Rei** *Centro* albergue ❼ continue down rua do Peregrino past pilgrim monument and over the N-547 which we cross several times today. We pass *A Casiña di Marcello* (left) and field of the pilgrims *Campo dos Romeiros* past [🚰] and back down to the N-547 and cross the Río Ruxián

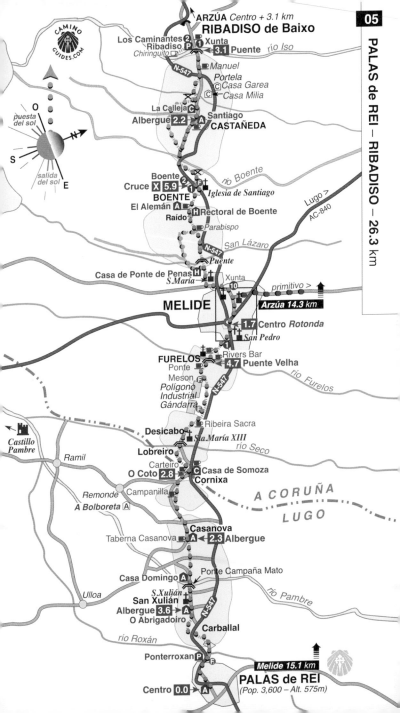

ARZÚA *Centro* + 3.1 km
RIBADISO de Baixo

Los Caminantes 2
Ribadiso P 1 Xunta
Chiringuito 3.1 Puente río Iso

Manuel
Portela
Casa Garea
Casa Milia

La Calleja C
Albergue 2.2 Santiago
CASTAÑEDA

Boente 2
Cruce X 5.9 1
BOENTE
El Alemán A
Raído H Rectoral de Boente
Parabispo
N-547 San Lázaro

Puente
Casa de Ponte de Penas H
S.María Xunta 10

MELIDE primitivo >
Arzúa 14.3 km

1.7 Centro *Rotonda*
San Pedro

Rivers Bar
FURELOS 4.7 Puente Velha
Ponte
Meson
Polígono
Industrial
Gándarra río Furelos

Ribeira Sacra
Desicabo Sta.María XIII
Lobreiro río Seco
Carteiro C Casa de Somoza
O Coto 2.8 Cornixa
Campanilla
Remonde A CORUÑA
A Bolboreta A LUGO

Casanova A 2.3 Albergue
Taberna Casanova

Casa Domingo A Ponte Campaña Mato
S.Xulián
San Xulián
Albergue 3.6 A N-547
O Abrigadoiro
Carballal
río Pambre

río Roxán

Ponterroxan P
Melide 15.1 km
PALAS de REI
Centro 0.0 A (Pop. 3,600 – Alt. 575m)

Lugo >
AC-840

CAMINO GUIDES.COM

O
puesta
del sol
S
salida
del sol
E

Castillo
Pambre

Ramil

Ulloa

up into **Carballal** with its raised granaries *Horreos* back down to re-cross the N-547 again onto the first of many delightful woodland paths into:

3.6 km San Xulián (*Xiao*) do Camiño classical camino village with its tiny XII[th]c church dedicated to Saint Julian and ●*Alb.* O Abrigadoiro *Priv.* *[18÷3]* €12 © 982 374 117 with dinner and breakfast available. Pass •*CR* La Pallota *x4* €70+ © 659 070 510. The path continues down to the rió Pambre that we cross at Ponte Campaña-Mato [**1.0** km] and ●*Alb.* Casa Domingo *Priv.***[21÷3]* €14 © 982 163 226 network* hostel part of an old mill occupying a tranquil rural setting on the rio Pambre with communal dinner. The route now climbs gently through ancient oak woods for [**1.3** km] to Mato-Casonova:

2.3 km Casanova ⅋ *Taberna Casanova* opp. ●*Alb.* Mato Casanova *Xunta.* *[20÷1]* €10 © 982 173 483 quiet woodland location on the border of Lugo and A Coruña. Continue up country lane to junction (left) ***Detour** off route (1½ km)* albergue and welcoming casa rural •*CR* Bolboreta *x8* €40+ © 609 124 717 traditional stone house by Vilar de Remonde with possibility to detour further to Pambre.

Detour: Castillo de Pambre. From *A Bolboreta* there is a 2.5 km (5 km return) designated walk by medieval bridge passing an ancient Celtic Castro to the impressive XIV[th]c Castillo de Pambre. Strategically situated on the río Pambre it has survived the advances of time and the Irmandiños revolt (the war in which the aristocracy were fighting the peasants rather than each other). The fight continues with disputes between private ownership and public access. Unlike its counterpart in Sarria, the four corner towers and inner keep are still proudly standing. 2 km further is the Palacio Villamayor de Ulloa one of the best-preserved Galician manor houses *Pazos*, family seat of the Ulloa's and setting for the novel *Los Pazos de Ulloa* by Emilia Pardo Bazán (only available in Spanish).

Continue up the Pass of the Oxen *Porto de Bois [scene of a bloody battle between warring nobility]* to the high point of this stage at 515m before crossing over the provincial border at scrap yard in Cornixa, past ☕ *Campanilla* in woodland setting; if busy continue to O Coto (0.7 km).

2.8 km O Coto with several ☕ *cafés* vying for the breakfast trade. Also •*P¨* Los dos Alemanes *x14* €25–€50 © 630 910 803 & •*CR¨* Casa de los Somoza *x10* €55+ © 981 507 372. We now follow an undulating track through woods to cross medieval bridge into the village of *field of hares* **Lobreiro** no facilities but the Romanesque Church of ***Santa María*** [**0.8** km] *XIII[th]c* with fine carved stone tympanum of Virgin and Child over the main door and opposite a former pilgrim hostel. We cross the medieval Magdalena Bridge over the río Seco into ***Desicabo***. The path continues up towards the main road and over a footbridge to join a stretch of senda separating the N-547 from an industrial estate *polígono industrial Gándara* [⌂] [**1.6** km]. Here the old *Orde de Caballeros y Damas del Camino de Santiago* have erected a monument to themselves and an enterprising young man established the welcoming ⚐ *Ribeira Sacra*. The path leads us back through woodland down to ⚐ *A Ponte Meson* at **Furelos [2.2 km]:**

4.7 km Furelos *Ponte Velha* medieval bridge into Furelos now a modern cafe nucleus with ⚐ *Rivers Bar* and •*P"Adro x3* €85. No trace remains of the medieval pilgrim hospital that adjoined *Igrexa San Juan* but the *Casa Museo* lends a sense of history. ⚐ *Taberna Farruco* [⚑] We begin the climb up to **Melide** through suburbs past the first of a dozen albergues *(Av. Price €12) Town Plan next page.* ❶Melide *Priv.[40÷2]* Ⓒ 627 901 552 *www. alberguemelide.com* entrance on Av. Lugo opp. •*H"Carlos x34* €25-55 Ⓒ 981 507 633. Keep s/o past •*CR* **A Lua do Camiño** *x8* €25-35 Ⓒ 6620 958 331 and ▮ *Casa Alongas V.* with terrace. Veer right> at ▮ *pizzeria Atenas* to join **main road N-547** at ▮ *pulperia A Garnacha.* Take next left for ❷Ezequiel *Priv.[18÷3]* Ⓒ 686 583 378 r/Sol,7. Romanesque Church of *San Pedro & San Roque* and XIV[th]c stone cross reputed to be the oldest in Galicia *Crucero do Melide.* To the rear Av. de la Habana @N°43 +200m •*Hs"Xaneiro x26* €45 Ⓒ 981 506 140. •*P El Molino x8* €25+ Ⓒ 981 506 048 c/Rosalía de Castro, 23. Pass variety of ▮/⚐ to ❸ **Arraigos** *Priv. [24÷1]* Ⓒ 646 343 370 Cantón de San Roque (main road) and laneway off •*P" Berenguela x12* €30-40 Ⓒ 981 505 417.

1.7 km Melide *Centro Ronda de la Coruña.* ❹ O Cruceiro *Priv.[80÷12]* Ⓒ 616 764 896 *www.alberguoocruceiro.es* ✣ *2 route options from central roundabout* (see map). ① *Direct* via r/San Pedro r/Principal past ❺ O Candil *Priv.[12÷2]* €15 Ⓒ 639 503 550 *www.ocandil.gal* and •*P Esquina x12* €40+ Ⓒ 981 505 802 c/Ichoas, 1. ② *Via Historic centre* Rua do Convento to **Concello** and ❶Turismo (museo). Detour 200m to ❻ **Alfonso II** *El Casto Priv.[30÷3]+* Ⓒ 981 506 454 *www.alberguealfonsoelcasto.com* Av. de Toques y Friol 52 (AC-840). To the rear of Capela S. Antonio on Praza Constitución: *Rua S.Antonio:* @N°6 ❼ San Antón *Priv.[36÷5]* Ⓒ 981 506 427 *www. alberguesananton.com* @N°14 •*P San Antón x 12* €35-50 Ⓒ 698 153 672 @ N°18 •*Pousada* Chiquitín *x 16* €30-50 Ⓒ 981 815 333 *www.chiquitinmelide. es* with modern roof terrace to rear @N°23 ❽ O Apalpador *Priv.[12÷2]* Ⓒ 679 837 969 adj. ❾ Melide *Xunta.[140÷6]* €10 Ⓒ 660 396 822.

Back on *N-547 Rua Progreso/ Codeseira* ❿ Pereiro *Priv.[40÷5]* +4 €40 Ⓒ 981 506 314 and ⓫ Montoto *Priv.[50÷4]* +1 €30 Ⓒ 646 941 887 *www. alberguemontoto.com* end of town •*P Sony x30* €40+ Ⓒ 981 505 473.

Other Lodging: *(AC-840)* •*P Orois x12* €40 Ⓒ 981 507 097 c/A. Boveda, 13. ▮/*P.* ♥ O Tobo do Lobo *x10* €35+ Ⓒ 981 507 773 c/Luis Seoane, 8, where chef Miguel delights to serve.

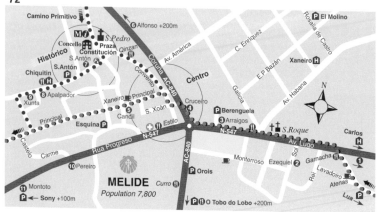

MELIDE: population 7,500 (declining) ❶*Turismo* (9:00-15:00) ✆ 981 505 003 *Casa Concello* Praza Convento. The old part of town follows its medieval layout of narrow winding streets with shops, bars and restaurants serving the regional speciality, octopus *pulpo*. In *Plaza del Convento* we find the austere parish church, Sancti Spiritus, formerly a XIVthc Augustinian monastery. Opp. is the original pilgrim refuge of 1502 *Antigo Hospital de Peregrinos* now a museum and information centre. Melide remains an important hub of the Jacobean pilgrimage and the point where pilgrims travelling down from Oviedo on the pilgrim route *camino Primitivo* join the *camino Francés*. Today's pilgrim facilities include a •*Masaje y fisioterapia* (servicio al peregrino) in c/Lavadoiro,18 ✆ 981 507 017 and hiking gear at • *Armeria Rua* ✆ 981 50 50 33 rua Convento 4 opp. popular ♙ *Casa Qinzan*.

Leave Melide via the western suburbs past *cementerio* [0.4 km] over N-547 (sign San Martiño) past Romanesque *Igrexa Santa María de Melide* XII *(photo)* [0.6 km]. Keep s/o to **option** [1.0 km]. ▲/[●●●● *Turn left for quiet alternative loop past •CR* **Ponte de Penas** *x10* €75+ ✆ 981 501 163 www.

casadapontedepenas.com *Continue over river and up onto woodland veering right in a wide arc back to the main route in Parabispo – similar distance].*

▲ For main route keep s/o into woodland over **río San Lázaro** [0.5 km] via stone causeway (leprosarium no longer visible). *[We cross several shallow river valleys during these final stages so our path is more undulating than the contour guide might suggest.]* We continue by path through shaded forest, oak and chestnut giving way to eucalyptus and pine. S/o through Carballal and the river beyond [1.6 km] through Parabispo ♙ *Taberna de Parabispo* and *El Pequeno Oasis* over río Raído and picnic area [2.2 km] to **Boente Arriba:** •CR **Rectoral de Boente** *x8* €85 ✆ 684 238 323 and ♙ ●*Alb.* El Alemán *[40÷4]* €16 ✆ 981 501 984 down to the N-547 [1.1 km] at:

5.9 km Boente *Cruce Igrexa Santiago* with image of the Saint above the altar and convivial parish priest who offers a blessing to passing pilgrims. *Alb.* ❶ **Boente** *Priv.[42÷4]* €14 *+6* €40+ © 981 501 974 + menú. ❷ **Fuente Saleta** *Priv.[22÷6]* €13 © 981 501 853 + menú (*also run bar Mandala in Arzua*) *Bar Bareta* + taxi (Nadia) © 680 686 391. We leave past *Cruceiro* and [📷] through underpass down into the Boente valley with shaded rest area (right), the riverside setting somewhat marred by the noise of traffic. Up the other side we join minor road N-547 (veers off right) and we climb to **option point** [**1.6** km] ▲. *[●●●● Turn left for quieter loop that bypasses Castañeda and rejoins the main route by rest area at rio Ribeiral – similar distance].*

▲ For main route keep s/o alongside road past 📷 *No Camino* and the parish Church of Santa María into Castañeda [**0.6** km]:

2.2 km Castañeda ●*Alb.* **Santiago** *Priv. [4÷1]* €13 *+1* €40 © 981 501 711 prominently located on the corner *A Fraga Alta* with attractive terrace bar and restaurant. *[It was here in Castañeda that the pilgrims would deposit the limestone rocks they had brought from Triacastela to be fired for the lime used in the building of the Cathedral at Santiago].* Just beyond the albergue we pass •*Apt.* **La Calleja** © 605 787 382 from €80 and down over river with shaded rest area [**0.6** km]. From here we go around a wooded hill with track (right) *[leads to N-547 and casa rurales ½ off route: •CR* **Garea** *x6* €50 © *981 500 400 and* •**Milía** *x8* €35+ © *981 515 241].* We now climb to alto (440m) and cross a raised pass over the N-547 [**1.0** km] through woodland to pick up minor road with 📷 *Manuel* [**0.6** km] down to the beautiful medieval bridge over the río Iso [**0.3** km] at Ribadiso da Baixo:

3.1 km Ribadiso *Alb.*❶ Ribadiso *Xunta.[60÷2]* €10 © 660 396 823 idyllic location on río Iso adj. medieval bridge. Fine reconstruction of one of the oldest pilgrim hospitals still in existence. Adj. 📷 *Meson Ribadiso* opp. the well restored •*P* **Ribadiso** €59+ © 981 500 703 and *Alb.* ❷ **Los Caminantes** *Priv.* *[68÷4]* €12 *+9* €30+ © 647 020 600 *www.albergueloscaminantes.com*.

[Detour 500m to delightful natural swimming and recreation area + 🍴/📷 *Chiringuito – see map].* **Note:** next albergues **Milpes / Miraiso** 0.9 km up steeply and next pension **O Retiro** 1.9 km. Plentiful accommodation in *Arzua* a full 3.2 km (a long way at the end of a long day). See next stage.

Personal Reflections:

06 RIBADISO – PEDROUZO (ARCA)
Santiago – 43.8 km (27.2 ml)

┄┄┄	--- ---	12.9 --- ---	54%
▬▬▬	--- ---	8.4 --- ---	36%
▬▬▬	--- ---	2.4 --- ---	10%
Total km		**23.7 km** (14.7 ml)	

Total ascent **1,150m** ±2 hrs
Alto.m ▲ Santa Irene **420m** (1,378 ft)
< Ⓐ Ⓗ > → Arzúa **3.1 km** →Salceda **14.1**
→ Santa Irene **20.0 km** →A Rua **21.7 km**.

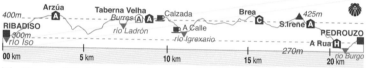

The Practical Path: over ½ this stage is on natural pathways with good shade offered by the ubiquitous eucalyptus. We start with a steep climb up into Arzúa and end with a gentle climb around the alto de Santa Irene. In between we have a largely level path with just 3 shallow river valleys.

The Mystical Path: *Let no one come to you without leaving better and happier.* Mother Teresa The memorial to Guillermo Watt is timely. What plans have *we* made for our onward journey? To contemplate the impermanence of our earthly form can be revitalising, urging us to make every step a prayer for understanding, every breath a song of gratitude, every moment a chance to awaken from the dream that keeps us separate from our eternal Source.

Personal Reflections: *"... The debate became heated, the only seeming accord being that the problems that beset our world were real and worsening. She had remained silent but now took the rare moment of quiet to state with utter conviction, 'There is only one solution'. Her words made us attentive – 'Allah'. The response was so unexpected. We had been looking for solutions on the level of the problem – our human condition of fear. She was a Sufi devotee. I note the paradox that it took a Muslim woman walking an outwardly Christian path to point out to us the deeper truth that lay beyond. Whatever name we choose to describe the ineffable is immaterial. The only way out of our dilemma, is inward through Love ..."*

0.0 km Ribadiso Continue up steeply along quiet road. S/o under N-547 *tunél* and right> past ●*Alb.* Milpes *Priv.[24÷3]* €12 ℗ 981 500 425 *www.alberguemilpes.com* and ●*Alb.* **Mirador** *Priv.[10÷2]*+ €12 ℗ 722 297 498 **[0.9** km] welcoming bar overlooking Ribadiso. Join main road which we follow all the way into **Arzua** *Entrada* **[1.0** km] at •*P‥*O **Retiro** *x18* €30+ €48 ℗ 981 500 554 and •*P* **Puerta de Arzúa** *x15* €45+ ℗ 9981 500 160.

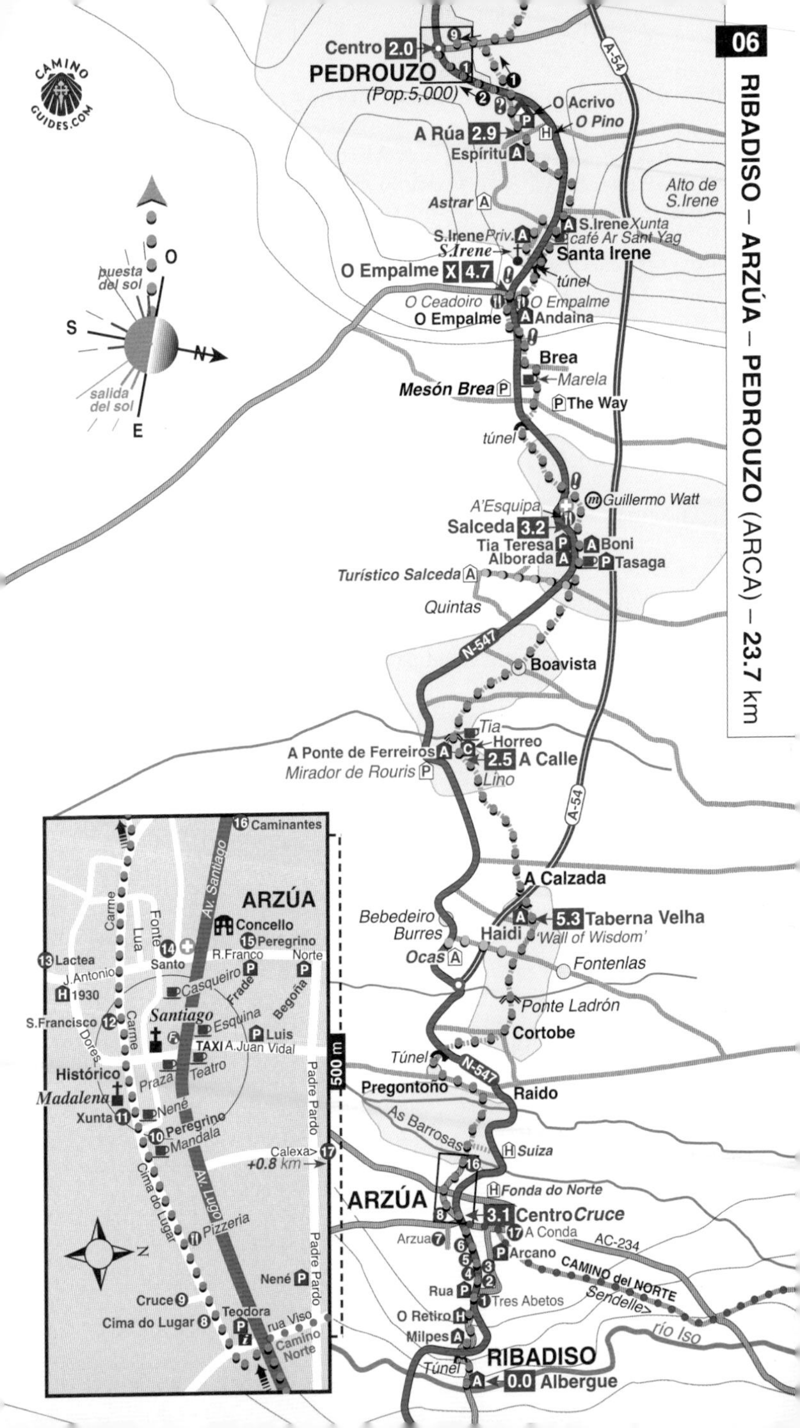

Centro **2.0**
PEDROUZO
(Pop.5,000)

9
1

1

2

1 O Acrivo
O Pino

A Rúa **2.9**
Espíritu **A**

P
H

Astrar **A**

*Alto de
S.Irene*

S.Irene Priv. **A**
S.Irene →
A S.Irene Xunta
café Ar Sant Yag

Santa Irene

O Empalme **X 4.7**
túnel

O Ceadoiro **1**
O Empalme
1 O Empalme
A Andaina

Brea
← *Marela*
Mesón Brea P

P The Way

túnel

A'Esquipa
m Guillermo Watt

Salceda 3.2
Tia Teresa
Alborada **A** **A** Boni
P Tasaga

Turístico Salceda **A**

Quintas

N-547

Boavista

Tia
Horreo
A Ponte de Ferreiros **A** **C** A Calle **2.5**
Mirador de Rouris P
Lino

A Calzada

Bebedeiro
Burres
A Taberna Velha **5.3**
Haidi *'Wall of Wisdom'*
Ocas **A**
Fontenlas

Ponte Ladrón
Cortobe

Túnel N-547
Pregontoño
Raido

As Barrosas
H *Suiza*

16
H Fonda do Norte
ARZÚA Centro *Cruce* **3.1**
8 **17** A Conda
Arzua **7** P Arcano AC-234
6
5
Rua **4** P **CAMINO del NORTE**
2 *Sendelle* →
3
O Retiro **H** **1** Tres Abetos
Milpes **A**
Túnel **RIBADISO**
A Albergue **0.0**
río Iso

ARZÚA inset map

16 Caminantes

13 Lactea
J.Antonio
H 1930
S.Francisco **12**

Carme
Fonte
Lúa
Av Santiago

ARZÚA
fi Concello
15 Peregrino
R.Franco P Norte
Casqueiro P Frade
14 Santo Esquina
Santiago
P Luis
TAXI A.Juan Vidal
Doroa
Carme
Histórico
Madalena Praza
Teatro
Xunta **11** Nené
10 Peregrino
Mandala
Oíma do Lugar
Av. Lugo
11 Pizzeria

Calexa→
+0.8 km **17**

Cruce **9**
Cima do Lugar **8**
Teodora
P
rúa Viso
Camiño
Norte
Nené P

Padre Pardo
500 m
Padre Pardo

Keep s/o to the first of ***17 Albergues (Av. Price €12-€15):***

Av. de Lugo: **Nº147** *Alb.*❶ **Los Tres Abetos** *Priv.[42÷5]* ✆ 649 771 142 www.tres-abetos.com @**Nº133** ❷ **Selmo** *Priv.[45÷1]* ✆ 981 939 018 www.oalberguedeselmo.com.@**Nº132** •*H*** **Arzúa** *x26* €60+ www.hotelarzua.com @ **Nº107** modern ❸ **Santiago Apóstol** *Priv.[90÷4]* ✆ 981 508 132.To rear on c/Castro, 6 •*P.* **Arcano** *x5* €24-36 ✆ 981 500 292. *(Left hand side)* @**Nº130** •*P*** **Rua** *x18* €30+ ✆ 981 500 139 www.pensionrua.com @**Nº133** ❹ **Don Quijote** *Priv.*[48÷4]* ✆ 981 500 139 adj. ❺ **Ultreia** *Priv.*[28÷1]* ✆ 981 500 471 network* hostel with ☕ & ❻ **Albergue de Camino** *Priv.[46÷4]+* ✆ 981 500 415 Keep s/o along the N-547 and off left on c/Rosalía de Castro and ❼ **Arzúa Turistico** *Priv.[12÷2] +4* €45 ✆ 981 508 233 and into the centre of town and popular 🍴/•*P*** **Teodora** *x28* €55+ ✆ 981 500 083 www.casateodora.com adj. ℹ***Turismo*** [**1.3** km]. ◆

3.1 km **Arzúa** ***Centro.*** The ***Camino del Norte*** joins from the right via rua do Viso and •*P** **Casa Nené** *x9* €60+ ✆ 981 505 107 c/Padre Pardo,24. ◆The waymarked route veers down left (parallel to the main road) into ***rúa Cima do Lugar*** @**Nº22** ❽ **Cima do Lugar** *Priv.[14÷1] +8* €40+ ✆ 661 663 669. @**Nº28** ❾ **Cruce De Caminos** *Priv.[56÷8]* ✆ 881 817 716 www.crucedecaminosarzua.com past 🍴 *pizzeria O Rueiro* @**Nº7** ❿ **Casa del Peregrino** *Priv.[14÷1]* ✆ 686 708 704 with 🍴 *A Taberna de Mera* to the rear on rua Calexa & finally @**Nº6** ⓫**Arzúa** *Xunta [56÷3]* €10 ✆ 660 396 824 (photo>) opp. ☕ *bar Mandala* where Josefina and Mariano tend to thirsty pilgrims adj. *Casa Nené* tranquil area that gets the evening sun. Here we find the XIVᵗʰc Augustinian ***capela da Madalena*** and 50m beyond we come to ***crossroads*** where other nearby lodging compete for the lucrative pilgrim trade.

Turn right for ☕ cafés around the central square in front of the modern Iglesia Santiago or see town plan embedded in stage map for location of the following accommodation: Beautifully restored ⓬**San Francisco** *Priv.[28÷2] +2* €40 ✆ 881 979 304 www.alberguesanfrancisco.com rear access to plaza, Rua Carmen, 18. ❒*Lavanderia automatica.* ⓭ **Vía Láctea** *Priv.[120÷12]* ✆ 981 500 581 www.alberguevialactea.com on r/José Antonio. ⓮**O Santo** *Priv.[22÷1]* ✆ 981 500 957 r/Xosé Neira Vilas, 4. ⓯ **Peregrino** *[20÷1]* ✆ 981 500 145 (mixed reports) r/ Norte, 7. ⓰ **Los Caminantes II** *Priv.[28÷1]* ✆ 647 020 600 Av. de Santiago, 14. + 800m ⓱ **A Conda** *Priv.[18÷1] +6* €45+ www.pensionvilarino.com c/Calexa, 92.

Other Lodging: ***Central:*** Recent renovation of the former pulperia O Conxuro •*H**** **1930 Boutique** *x14* €90 ✆ 670 784 787 www.1930boutiquehotel.com r/ Dores, 19. On rúa Ramón Franco •*P** **Casa Frade** *x6* €50+ ✆ 981 500 019 /

adj. •*P* Casa Carballeira *x15* €50 © 981 500 094. Above the offices of BBVA the popular •*P* Begoña © 981 500 517. Further out •*H* A Fonda do Norte *x10* €40-50 © 654 930 254 modern hotel +800m. •*H* Suiza *x25* €45-65 © 981 500 908 off route + 400m on main road N-547.

ARZÚA pop: 6,300. ❶ *Turismo* Praza do Peregrino © 981 508 056. The modern town overshadows its medieval core. The noisy central square has a variety of bars, cafés and restaurants and the modern parish church dedicated to St. James with image of Santiago as both Moorslayer and pilgrim. Arzúa is known for its local cheese and the cheese fair *festa do queixo* held in March. The camino continues out through the old quarter of town down c/del Carmen past fountain and over stream (site of San Lázaro hospice) onto a delightful track through ancient oak woods in *As Barrosas* (track to Hotel Suiza right) meandering over several small streams onto side road into *Preguntoño* to *tunél* [2.7 km] under the N-547. We now alternate between country lanes & gravel tracks through the hamlets of *Raído* and *Fontelas* [2.0 km] [*Detour: 0.8 km to:* ●*Alb.* Camiño das Ocas *Priv.* [30÷6] €12 +4 €40 © 648 404 780 www.caminodasocas.com on the N-547 in *Burres*]. Dense woodland brings us to **Taberna Velha** [0.6 km].

5.3 km Taberna Velha with its 'Wall of Wisdom' (depending on ones perspective) and Haidi's discreet ●*Alb.* Taberna Velha *Priv.* [8÷1] €17 © 687 543 810. Also 🍴 *bar TabernaNova* serving fresh local produce in a blend of Spanish and American home cooking. Continue over new autopista into **A Calzada** [1.0 km]. The next village **A Calle** [1.5 km] has 2 other cafés with w.c.'s!

2.5 km A Calle quintessential camino village with 🛏 *Lino* also 🛏 *Casa Tia Dolores* [🚿] by the river. Pass •*CR* do Horreo *x6* €60 © 626 616 758. ●*Alb.* A Ponte de Ferreiros *Priv.* [30÷2] €15 © 665 641 877 Pilar. [*300m off route* •*P* Mirador de Rouris *x8* €40 © 608 981 630 *far side of* N-547. Also *Meson As Brasas*]. Gravel track to **Boavista** [1.8 km] *Casa Boavista* and 🛏 *'Portraits'* with peaceful terrace and enterprising (if touristy) photo gallery. Continue past 🍴*Bar Brea* and crossroads ✛ [*Detour:* ●*Alb.* Turístico Salceda *Priv.* [8÷1] €15 +15 €47 © 981 502 767 + 🍴🛏 *menú V.* ½ km the **far** side of the N-547]. ✛ Continue s/o to *Salceda* [1.4 km] on the noisy N-547.

3.2 km Salceda with 🛏 *Casa Verde* (T-shirt bar!) •*P* Tasaga *x6* €50 © 981 113 077. ●*Alb.* Alborada *Priv.* [10÷1] €15 +4 €55 © 620 151 209. ●*Alb.* La Corona *Priv.* [20÷6] €15 © 981 073 382. •*P* Tía Teresa €45 © 628 558 716 🍴 *Mesón A'Esquipa* with garden & ➕Farmacia. Continue on woodland path with monument (right) to pilgrim *Guillermo Watt* who died at this spot only a day away from his earthly destination. A pedestrian **underpass** [2.6 km] brings us into **Brea** [0.2 km]. S/o down to junction ✛ [*Detour: left 100m far side of N-547* •*P* O Mesón Brea *x6* €30+ 🛏 S.Miguel © 981 511 040]. S/o to join path by **main road** [0.8 km]. **O Pino** •*H* O Pozo *x5* €50+ © 674 047 598. Cross over the N-547 [!] past N-547 'rest' area and up to crossroads [1.1 km].

4.7 km **O Empalme** ***Cruce*** 🍴 *O Ceadoiro* menú. *[!]* Cross N-547 again to 🍴/●*Alb.* **Andaina** *Priv.[15÷4]* €12 ✆ 981 502 925. Continue s/o up onto track through woods around *Alto de Santa Irene.* Continue down to ***túnel*** [**0.8** km] s/o for Xunta albergue or continue left via underpass to *Fonte y capela Santa Irene* [**0.4** km] *(an early Christian martyr)* up to: **Santa Irene** [**1.2** km] pass temporarily closed ●*Alb.* **Santa Irene** *Priv.* [32÷2]* €14 ✆ 981 511 000 network* hostel. *[**Detour:** 700m off route:* ●*Alb.* **Rural Astar** *Priv.[24÷5] €14* ✆ *608 092 820].* Continue back down and cross N-547 past pilgrim rest area [🚰] & ☕ *Ar Sant Yag* to ●*Alb.* **Santa Irene** *Xunta. [32÷2] €8* directly on the busy main road (noisy). Continue down on woodland path through underpass (2) into **A Rúa** [**1.7** km].

2.9 km **A Rúa** quiet, traditional hamlet with ●*Alb.* **Espíritu Xacobeo** *[32÷2]* €12 +*3* €60 ✆ 620 635 284 www.espirituxacobeo.com. •*H** **O Pino** *x15* ✆ *981 511 035 on main road].* •*CR* **O Acivro** *x10* €75+ ✆ 981 511 316 + 🍴/☕ and garden. Pass ▲**Camping Peregrino O Castiñeiro** tents €12 ✆ 981 197 125 www.campingperegrino.es. Continue over río Burgo to climb steeply up to the N-547 **Opción** [**0.7** km]: To access **Pedrouzo** ***direct*** **Ⓐ** turn left up the main road N-547 to:

2.0 km **Pedrouzo** ***Centro*** *(parish* ***Arca*** *municipality* ***O Pino****)* Satellite town of Santiago straddling the N-547 with variety of shops and restaurants. Wide range of lodging mostly on the N-547. 9 albergues (Av. price €12+): ❶ **O Burgo** *Priv.*[14÷1]+5* €40 ✆ 630 404 138 www.albergueoburgo.es adj. Repsol. ❷ **Arca** *Xunta.[150÷4] €10 (down behind the supermercado off the N-457) (photo>).* ❸ **Mirador** *[50÷7]* €15 ✆ 686 871 215 www.alberguemiradordepedrouzo.com ***Town centre:*** ❹ **Porta de Santiago** *Priv.*[54÷2]* ✆ 981 511 103 www.portadesantiago.com ☕ and rear patio. Opp. ❺ **O Trisquel** *Priv.[78÷6]* ✆ 616 644 740 corner of Rúa do Picon. ❻ **Edreira** *Priv.*[40÷4]* ✆ 981 511 365 www.albergue-edreira.com purpose-built network* hostel Rúa da Fonte 19. ❼ **REMhostel** *Priv.[50÷2]* ✆ 981 510 407. Adj'. ❽ **Cruceiro** *Priv. [94÷6]* ✆ 981 511 371 www.alberguecruceirodepedrouzo.com (facilities incl. sauna) on Av. Iglesia in modern block of apartments.

Other Lodging €30-70: ***Central*** on N-547: •*P* **Compás** *x11* ✆ 981 511 309. •*Hs*** **Platas** *x24* ✆ 981 511 378. Adj. (rear) •*P.* **A Solaina** *x12* ✆ 633 530 918 Rúa Picón, 3. •*P** **Rosella** *x6* ✆ 600 350 346. •*P** **Una Estrella Dorada** *x4* ✆ 630 018 363. ***Av. de Santiago:*** •*P* **9 de Abril** *x4* ✆ 606 764 762. •*P** **Pedrouzo** *x14* ✆ 671 663 375 www.pensionpedrouzo.com. •*P* **Noja** *x12* ✆ 627 127 696. •*P** **Codesal** *x7* ✆ 981 511 064 rua Codesal. •*Pr** **Muiño** *x10* ✆ 981 511 144. •*Pr** **Maribel** *x5* ✆ 609 459 966 adj. •*P* **Arca** *x7* ✆ 657 888 594. •*P* **LO** *x12* ✆ 981 510 401.

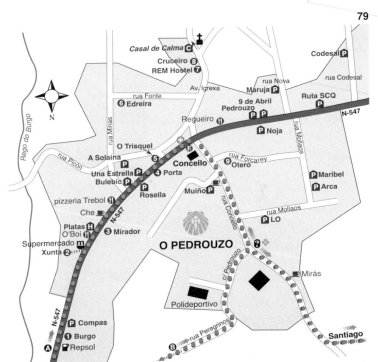

❸ If you are continuing directly to Santiago continue s/o over the N-547 onto woodland path merging into rúa Peregrino past sports hall *polideportivo* to **T-Junction [1.0** km]: ❖ *[path to Santiago continues right]*. To access the rear of Pedrouzo **[0.3** km] turn <left into rua Concello passing the delightful ●*P˙***O Muiño** *x7* (Mayka) ℂ 981 511 144 *www.pensión-o-muiño.es* with quiet garden to rear adj. 🛌 *bar O Muiño* & *Alb.* **❾ Otero** *Priv.[34÷2]* ℂ 671 663 374 *www.alberguemotero.com* with terrace on c/Forcarei, 2. Continue s/o to *Concello (1.3 km).* and centre of Pedrouzo [⛪]:

Note: *If you intend to make the cathedral for 12 noon pilgrim mass you need to leave early in the morning. Note also new security measures prohibit backpacks inside the cathedral so you need time to check into your lodging or the new pilgrim office which is 300m from the cathedral and also has security systems which can cause lengthy delays. 'Pilgrim Services' Rua Nova 7 adj. cathedral south door stores backpack for €3. A less stressful option may be to visit the cathedral later in the day*

Personal Reflections:

07 O PEDROUZO (ARCA) – SANTIAGO
Santiago 20.1 km *(12.5 ml)*

	8.0	*40%*
	7.7	*38%*
	4.4	*22%*
Total km	**20.1 km** *(12.5 ml)*	

Total ascent **720m** *±1¼ hr*
Alto ▲ Monte do Gozo **370 m** *(1,214 ft)*
< Ⓐ Ⓗ > ➲Amenal **3.4 km** ➲Lavacolla **9.5 km** ➲Monte Gozo **15.2 km**.

[elevation profile: 400m — Aeropuerto 410m T.G.V — Monte Gozo 380m — PEDROUZO 300m — S.Paio — rego Covo — Vilamaior — San Marcos — SANTIAGO — rego Amenal 200m — río Sionlla — Lavacolla — San Lázaro — 00 km / 5 km / 10 km / 15 km / 20]

The Practical Path: Almost half this final stage is on delightful woodland paths; make the most of their shade and the peace they exude. As we get nearer the city, asphalt and crowds begin to take over as bus loads of pilgrims join the route for this one day into Santiago. If you are making for the pilgrim mass at 12 noon be prepared for large crowds and try and create an air of compassionate detachment. Be patient and prepare for the long slog up to Monte Gozo which, while surrounded by woodland, is all on asphalt.

The Mystical Path: *He went up into the mountain to pray... and the fashion of his countenance was altered, and his raiment was white and glistening. Luke IX, 29.* Will you stay awhile and lose yourself in the tiny grove of holm oak, itself almost lost amongst the mass of alien eucalyptus? Will you stop in Lavacolla, whose waters were used in the ritual cleansing of pilgrims prior to entering the holy City? Today the water is putrid but it is the symbolic purification that we seek so that we might glisten with the pure white light of consciousness.

Personal Reflections: *"... I could find no joy on this hill amongst the crowds huddled against the driving rain ... As I entered the cathedral I realised I had failed in my purpose. But in that same instant I realised I had been searching in the wrong place. A sudden rush of joy enveloped my soaking body. I knew the answer lay where the world of things ended and the unseen world began and I knew I had to go there. I hurried down the steps and out the city. I was alone but I had company. I did not know where I was going but I felt completely guided ..."*

0.0 km O Pedrouzo *Centro* [⛪] Turn up rua Concello past sports hall *polideportivo* **[0.3 km]** *(camino from A Rua joins from the right)*. S/o past ⬛*Mirás* and <left into eucalyptus forest through San Antón down into the río Amenal valley over rio Amenal and under N-547 *túnel* **[3.0 km]:**

● *Compostela Inn*
← (+7.1 km)

E-1
AC-841
AP-9
N-525

CAMINO
GUIDES.COM

Seminario Belvis **13**

Santos **10** **12**

1.0 Catedral
1.6 Cruceiro San Pedro
SANTIAGO
DE COMPOSTELA

A Fonte **4**
Fin del Camino **3**

9
8
7
6 Santo Santiago
5

Capilla San Lázaro
Dream

2.3 San Lázaro
2 Dream
H San Jacobo
1 San Lázaro

Monte de Gozo
Albergue **2.0** → **A**

Capilla S.Marcos
Monte del Gozo ▲ **A**
370m A Chisca ■ **H** Akelarre

San Marcos

Camping *S.Marcos* **3.7**

Camping
▲
410m
▲
TVG

Casa de Amancio **C**
Villamaior

† *Capilla S.Roque*
H San Paio
2.2 Lavacolla *igrexa*

Lavacolla → **A**

Ruta Jacobeo → **H**
Garcas **H**

túnel

H The Last 12k
Porta de Santiago
3.9 San Paio

Lavacolla aeropuerto
Rosalía de Castro

✈ ✈

A Pereira ◯

A-54
AP-9
E-1

N-634a

N-634

Cimadevila
Amenal **H**
3.4 Amenal *túnel*

O
S N
E

San Antón

(ARCA - O PINO)
O PEDROUZO
Centro **0.0** →

8
polideportivo

N-547

3.4 km Amenal *túnel* •*H¨* Amenal *x13*
€60+ Ⓒ 981 510 431 with popular ☕ and
•*P.*Kilómetro 15 *x4* €50 Ⓒ 981 897 086.
Continue up woodland path through
Cimadevila. A forest track brings us
around the perimeter of Santiago airport
to motorway roundabout and down

into a deep cutting at the end of the runway. Here personal items have been
discarded as symbol of renewal as we cross over an access road into:

3.9 km San Paio ancient hamlet with ☕ *Casa Porta de Santiago* and •*P¨***The
Last Twelve** *x6* €60+ Ⓒ 619 904 743. We now enter the last recognisable
stretch of the medieval 'Royal Way' *Real Camino* as we head uphill veering
right> onto a natural path lined with remnants of the deciduous woodland
that once covered this area before eucalyptus was imported to fuel the pulp
industry. Head downhill passing rear entrance to •*H¨***Ruta Jacobea** *x20* €90
Ⓒ 981 888 211 to:

2.2 km Lavacolla *Igrexa* [⌂] ☕/•*P* **A Concha** *x12* €30 Ⓒ 981 888 390.
•*P* **Dorotea** *x18* €50 Ⓒ 619 424 969. ●*Alb.* **A Fábrica** *Priv.[32÷1]* €20 Ⓒ
681 075 647. •*P* **San Paio** *x45* €38-50 Ⓒ 981 888 205. •*P* **Xacobeo** *x4* €55
Ⓒ 608 363 658. Lavacolla is historically the place where medieval pilgrims
came to wash *lavar* and purify themselves before entering the city. Due to
the international airport (Santiago Rosalía de Castro) modern Lavacolla
now caters more for the business traveller than the pilgrim with variety of
restaurants, bars and hotels.

[Detour Capela San Roque 300m]: *If you continue down the steps past the
bandstand you come to the chapel dedicated to the pilgrim saint San Roque].*
The path now continues around the side of the parish church and past ●*Alb.*
Lavacolla *Priv.[32÷1]* €13 Ⓒ 981 897 274. Also on main road •*H** **Garcas**
x61 €35-50 Ⓒ 981 888 225 (+500m). Cross over N-634a over a small stream
to head steeply uphill on dedicated track through crossroads at **Villamaior**
[1.4 km] and past ☕/•**Casa de Amancio** Ⓒ 981 897 086 apartments €70+.
Continue on pilgrim track down over a stream with rest area and up to our
high point today at 410m *[not Monte de Gozo but the studios of TV Galicia!].*
Turn <left at T-jct ☕/▲ *San Marcos* **[2.2 km]:**

3.7 km **Camping** *San Marcos*. Continue down side of RTVE into **San**
Marcos with several ☕ *bars/cafés.* **[200m** *off* route s/o •*H* **Akelarre** *x12*
€45 Ⓒ 981 552 689 *on the N-634].* Turn <left up rua San Marcos past ☕
A Chica. Turn <left for modern ●*Alb.***Juan Pablo II** *[68÷3]*+ €10 Ⓒ 981
597 222 (+350m). For Santiago continue s/o along short paved path to the
enchanting *capilla de San Marcos* (mass daily 19:30) in a glade of trees with
☕ *Cantina* and where medieval pilgrims espied the cathedral towers (the
first one being crowned 'king' for the day) and giving rise to an exclamation,
'Mount of Joy' *Monte do Gozo.* Continue s/o downhill to:

2.0 km Monte del Gozo ●*Alb.*Monte do Gozo *Xunta.[500÷120]* €10 +*100* €35 dbl. ©881 255 386 *www.montedogozo.com* with beds in separate blockhouses (4-8 beds in each room). Good modern facilities with ⊪/🍴 *bar, restaurant* and large canteen on the main plaza. The hill itself has been reshaped to provide a vast leisure complex for the city. The sprawling buildings are the price of an ever-increasing demand for accommodation. The tiny chapel of San Marcos is the only building left on the hill that gives any sense

of the history of this place. The camino continues down Rúa do Peregrino and flight of steps where we join the city traffic to pass over railway line and past statue of *El Templario Peregrino* (left) over A-9 autopista and roundabout into the wide N-634 and modern city suburbs where we pass the prominent monument to notable historical figures connected with the camino.

At the 2nd **roundabout** [**1.6** km] on opp. side of the road behind *Museo Pedagóxico Alb.* ❶ San Lázaro *Xunta.[80÷6]* €10 ©981 571 488 – bus #6 to centre. Continue on the main road past •*H'* San Jacobo *x20* €37+ © 981 580 361 *www.hotelsanjacobo.com* and ❷ Dream in Santiago *Priv.[60÷6]* © 981 943 208 *www.dreaminsantiago.com* opp. 🍴 *Dreams.* Over roundabout passing chapel of ***San Lázaro Santiago*** [**0.6** km] *[witness to the leprosarium that existed here in the XII[th]c, sufficiently far outside the medieval city walls to ensure contamination didn't spread inside].* 100m later we come to major crossroads (ruas S. Lázaro & Roma) and albergue option [**0.1** km]

2.3 km San Lázaro *[albergues generally open early so you can unload backpacks and shower before visiting the city. Backpacks are **not** allowed in the cathedral].* ❖ *(200m left–signposted)* ❸ Fin del Camino *Asoc.[112÷8]* €12 © 981 587 324 c/Moscova corner r/Roma, modern building behind the *Policía* good facilities *(bus 11 to Plaza Galicia).* ❖ Continue s/o into ▌Rúa do Valiño *[where 'below' the park (steep steps left)]:* ❹ A Fonte *Priv.[30÷1]* © 881 290 468 *www.alberguesafonte.com* Rúa Estocolmo. Keep s/o to Nº3 ❺ Santo Santiago *Priv.[40÷3]* €10-12 © 657 402 403 adj. •*H* S.Lazaro *x31* €40+ © 981 584 344. Pass viewpoint into ▌Rúa das Fontiñas Nº65 ❻ Monterey *Priv.[36÷3]* €15+ © 655 484 299 s/o into ▌Rúa da Fonte dos Concheiros Nº13 (corner of r/Altiboia) ❼ La credencial *Priv.[36÷3]* €14+ © 639 966 704. @ Nº2c ❽ SCQ *Priv.[24÷4]* €18+ © 622 037 300 ❾ Sixtos no Caminho *Priv.[40÷1]* €15-20 © 881 024 195 *www.alberguesixtos.com* (corner of Av.Lugo). Cross ring road*! Av. de Lugo* (old bus station *estación de autobuses* – up right) into ▌Rúa dos Concheiros *[named after the medieval stall holders here who sold shells **conchas** to arriving pilgrims].*

Continue up to Nº48 ❿ Santos *Priv.[24÷3]* © 881 169 386. Nº36 ⓫ La Estrella *Priv.[24÷1]* © 881 973 926 *www.laestrelladesantiago.es* Nº10

⑫ Porta Real *Priv.[20÷1]* ⓒ 633 610 114 *www.albergueportareal.es* Continue up to **Cruceiro de San Pedro** which heralds our arrival into the old city with the spires of the Cathedral ahead and option to go direct to main hostel.

1.6 km San Pedro ❖ ***Option:*** shortcut to main hostel at Av. Quiroga Palacios Belvís **+500**m. Note access from city centre via rua Trompas (see city plan) **⑬ Seminario Menor** *Conv.[170÷30]*€16 *+81* €22-44 ⓒ 881 031 768 *www. alberguesdelcamino.com* Depending on time of arrival consider going directly to the hostel (Reception opens 08:00 rooms from 13.30) *Directions*: Turn left into r/ Corredoira das Fraguas by 🛒 *Dia%* supermarket (imm. before *Cruceiro de San Pedro*) and keep s/o direct to Convento de Belvís and Seminario Menor which houses the main city hostel above Parque Belvís *(extensive park which gets the evening sun)*.

❖ For the cathedral continue down rua de San Pedro past the Church of San Pedro & Praza (left) and s/o to the famous Gate of the Way **Porta do Camiño** which gives access to the wonderful old city. Up on the right overlooking the **Porta do Camiño** Convento de Santo Domingo de Bonaval housing the Panteón and Galician museum, with the centre for contemporary Galician art opp. There is a quiet park behind the convent buildings to refresh body and soul from the rigours of city life. (See city map for directions to these and other places of interest). We now proceed up Casas Reais and Rúa das Ánimas into Praza de Cervantes (with bust of the writer atop the central pillar) now we head down rúa da Azabachería (lined with jewellers selling jet *azabache* – see later) into Praza da Inmaculada (also called Azabachería) down under the arch of the **Pazo do Xelmírez** to:

1.0 km Praza Obradoiro *Catedral.* Take time to *arrive.* We each experience different emotions, from euphoria to disappointment, on seeing the Cathedral. Whatever your individual reaction, honour and accept it. Gratitude for safe arrival is a frequent response but if you are overwhelmed by the crowds why not return later when you feel more composed and the Cathedral is, perhaps, quieter (open daily from 07:00 until 21:00). Whether now or later and whichever door you entered by, you might like to follow the timeworn pilgrim ritual as follows:

[1] Due to erosion it is no longer permitted to place your hand in the Tree of Jesse, the central column of the Master Mateo's masterpiece Door of Glory *Portico de Gloria*. But you can stop and admire the incomparable beauty of this inner portico carved between 1166 and 1188 (the exterior façade was added in 1750). The Bible and its main characters come alive in this remarkable storybook in stone. The central column has Christ in Glory flanked by the apostles and, directly underneath, St. James sits as intercessor

between Christ and the pilgrim. Millions of pilgrims over the centuries have worn finger holes in the solid marble as a mark of gratitude for their safe arrival, the reason why it is now protected by a barrier. Proceed to the other side and where pilgrims of the past would touch their brow to that of Maestro Mateo, whose kneeling figure is carved into the back of the central column (facing the altar) and received some of his artistic genius in the ritual known as head-butting the saint *Santo d'Os Croques*. Proceed to the High Altar (right) to ascend the stairs and [2] hug the Apostle. Perhaps lay your head on his broad shoulders and say what you came here to say. Proceed down the steps on the far side to the crypt and the reliquary chapel under the altar. [3] Here, you can kneel before the casket containing the relics of the great Saint and offer your prayer ...

Pilgrim mass currently takes place four times per day; 07:30 / 09:30 / 12:00 / 19:30 (doors may close 5 minutes before on busy days). The swinging of the giant incense burner *Botafumeiro* was originally used to fumigate the sweaty (and possibly disease-ridden) pilgrims. The ritual requires half a dozen attendants *tiraboleiros* to perform it so has become a more infrequent event, details of special occasions when the *Botafumeiro* will be used can be found on the cathedral website (*www.catedraldesantiago.es*). You may also chance upon the spectacle if you happen to be in mass on a day when a private party has paid for the ritual to be performed, though these dates are not available in advance. The seating capacity has been extended to 1,000 so you might even find somewhere to sit but don't hold any expectations and remember – time itself is a journey.

Personal Reflections:

Four squares surround the cathedral and provide access to it, as follows:

Praza do Obradoiro. The 'golden' square of Santiago is usually thronged with pilgrims and tourists admiring the dramatic west facing façade of the Cathedral, universal symbol of Santiago, with St. James looking down on all the activity from his niche in the central tower. This provides the main entrance to the Cathedral and the Portico de Gloria. To the right of the steps is the discrete entrance to the museum. A combined ticket will provide access to all rooms including the

crypt and the cloisters and also to the XIIthc palace of one of Santiago's most famous individuals and first archbishop, Gelmírez *Pazo de Xelmírez* situated on the (left). In this square we also find the beautiful Renaissance façade of the Parador named after Ferdinand and Isabel *Hostal dos Reis Católicos* on whose orders it was built in 1492 as a pilgrim hospice. Opposite the Cathedral is the more austere neoclassical seat of various government bodies and town hall *Pazo de Raxoi* with its solid arcade. Finally, making up the fourth side of the square is the gable end of the *Colegio de S. Jerónimo* part of the university. Moving anti-clockwise around the cathedral – turn up into Rúa de Fonseca to:

Praza das Praterías. The most intimate of the squares with its lovely centrepiece, an ornate statue of horses leaping out of the water. On the corner of Rúa do Vilar we find the Dean's House *Casa do Deán* formerly the pilgrim office. Along the walls of the Cathedral itself are the silversmith's *plateros* that give the square its name. Up the steep flight of steps we come to the magnificent southern door to the Cathedral, the oldest extant doorway and traditionally the entrance taken by pilgrims coming from Portugal. The quality of the carvings and their arrangement

is remarkable and amongst the many sculptured figures is one of St. James between two cypress trees. Continuing around to the right we come to:

Praza da Quintana. This wide square is identified by the broad sweep of steps separating the lower part *Quintana of the dead* from the upper *Quintana of the living*. Opp the Cathedral is the wall of the *Mosteiro de San Paio de Antealtares* (with museum of sacred art). The square provides the eastern entrance to the Cathedral via the Holy Gate *Porta Santa* sometime referred to as the Door

of Pardon *El Perdón* only opened during Holy Years. Adjoining it is the main entrance to the Cathedral shop that has several guidebooks (in various languages) with details of the Cathedral's many chapels and their interesting carvings and statuary and the priceless artefacts and treasures in the museum. Finally, we head up the broad flight of steps around the corner and back into:

Praza da Inmaculada (Azabachería) to the north facing Azabachería façade, with the least well-known doorway and the only one that *descends* to enter the Cathedral. Opposite the cathedral is the imposing southern edifice of *Mosteiro de San Martiño Pinario* the square in front gets any available sun and attracts street artists. The archbishop's arch *Arco Arzobispal* brings us back to the Praza do Obradoiro.

The **Pilgrim Office** *Oficina del Peregrino* now at rua Carretas *below the parador* ℂ 981 568 846 open daily 09:00-21:00 (10:00-20:00 winter). The new office has tight security procedure (expect lengthy delays). It lacks the informal atmosphere of the former office in rua Vilar with its team of *Amigos*. However, providing you have fulfilled the criteria of a bona fide pilgrim and walked at least the last 100 km (200 km on bike or horseback) for religious/ spiritual reasons and collected 2 stamps per day on your *credencial* you will be awarded the *Compostela* which may entitle you to certain privileges such as reduced entry fees to museums and a free meal at the Parador! If you do not fulfil the criteria you may still be able to obtain a ***certificado*** (€3) which is essentially a certificate of distance travelled. The welcoming Companions meet in a room upstairs and in the adjoining chapel (see below).

• **The Camino Chaplaincy** offers Anglican services Sundays 12.30 at Igrexa de Santa Susana, parca da Alameda.

• **Camino Companions** based within the Pilgrims Office, offer reflective prayer in the pilgrims office *chapel* 11:30 and reflection and integration room 6, 1st floor 15:00 (both daily Mon-Sat). Mass in English daily (excl. Wednesdays) 10:30 also in the *chapel*.

• **Pilgrim House** rua Nova 19 also offers a place of welcome and reflection 11:00–20:00 (closed Wed & Sun) under the care of Terra Nova USA.

● **Pilgrim's Reception Office** Rúa das Carretas, 33. © 981 568 846 (*09:00-19.00*) ❶ **Turismo** *Centro*: r/ Vilar 63 © 981 555 129 *May-Oct: 09:00-19.00 (winter 17:00)* ● **Laundromat:** 09:00-22:00 **SC18** Rúa San Clemente 18 © 673 753 869. ● **Consignia Praca Quintana** (09:00-21:00) backpack storage €3 per day opp. Cath.● **Intermodal Central Train/Bus Station** 700m (10 mins) South of Praza Galicia.

● *Albergues: €15-€25* (*depending on season / beds per dormitory*) ❶–⓭ (*see page 83*). ▌ c/ **S.Clara** ⓮ **LoopINN** (*La Salle*) © 981 585 667 ▌ c/ **Basquiños Nº45** ⓯ *Basquiños* (*closed*) Nº67 ⓰ **Meiga Backpackers** *Priv.*[*30÷5*] © 981 570 846 *www.meiga-backpackers.es.* ◀**Centro Histórico:** ⓱ O Fogar de Teodomiro *Priv.*[*20÷5*]+ © 981 582 920 Plaza de Algalia de Arriba 3. ⓲ The Last Stamp *Priv.*[*62÷10*] © 981 563 525 r/ Preguntorio 10. ⓳ Azabache *Priv.*[*20÷5*] © 981 071 254 c/Azabachería 15. ⓴ Km.0 *Priv.*[*50÷10*] © 881 974 992 *www.santiagokm0.es* r/ Carretas 11 (new renovation by pilgrim office) ㉑ Blanco *Priv.*[*20÷2*]+4 €35-55 © 881 976 850 r/ Galeras 30. ㉒ Mundoalbergue *Priv.*[*34÷1*] © 981 588 625 c/ San Clemente 26. ㉓ *Roots & Boots* (*closed*) *Priv.*[*48÷6*] © 699 631 594 r/Campo Cruceiro do Galo. ◀*Otros:* ㉔ La Estación *Priv.*[*24÷2*] © 981 594 624 r/ Xoana Nogueira 14 (adj. rail station **+2.9** km). ㉕ Compostela Inn *Priv.*[*120÷30*]+ © 981 819 030 off *AC-841* (*+6.0 km*). ● *Hoteles €30–60:* •*Hs* Moure © 981 583 637 r/dos Loureiros. •*H* Fonte S. Roque © 981 554 447 r/do Hospitalillo 8. •*P* Linares [*14÷2*] © 981 943 253 •*Hs* Estrela © 981 576 924 Plaza de San Martín Pinario 5. •*Hs* **San Martín Pinario** *x127* © 981 560 282 *www. hsanmartinpinario.com* Praza da Inmaculada. •**Pico Sacro** r/San Francisco 22 © 981 584 466. •*H*** Montes © 981 574 458 r/ Raíña 11. **Rúa Fonseca Nº1** •*P* Fonseca © 603 259 337. **Nº5** •*Hs* Libredon 981 576 520 & •*P* Barbantes /Celsa ©981 583 271 on r/ Franco 3. **Rúa Vilar Nº8** •*H***Rua Villar © 981 519 858. Nº17** •*H*** Airas Nunes © 981 569 350. **Nº65** •*Hs*** Suso © 981 586 611. **Nº76** •*Hs* Santo Grial © 629 515 961. •Anosa Casa © 981 585 926 r/ Entremuralles 9 adj. •*Hs* Mapoula © 981 580 124. •*Hs* Alameda © 981 588 100 San Clemente 32. ◀*€60–90:* •*H* A Casa Peregrino © 981 573 931 c/ Azabachería. •Entrecercas © 981 571 151 r/Entrecercas. **Porta de Pena Nº17** •*H* Costa Vella © 981 569 530 (+ Jardín) **Nº5** •*P* Casa Felisa © 981 582 602 (+Jardín). •MV Algaia © 981 558 111 Praza Algalia de Arriba 5. •*H*** Pazo De Altamira © 981 558 542 r/ Altamira, 18. ◀*€100+* •*H*** San Francisco Campillo de San Francisco © 981 581 634. •*H*** Hostal de los Reyes Católicos (Parador) Plaza Obradoiro © 981 582 200.

Centro Histórico: ❶ Convento de Santo Domingo de Bonaval XIIIth (*panteón de Castelao, Rosalía de Castro y museo do Pobo Galego*). ❷ Mosteiro de San Martín Pinario XVIth *y museo* ❸ Pazo de Xelmirez XIIth ❹ Catedral XIIth–XVIIIth *Portica de Gloria, claustro, museo e tesouro* ❺ Hostal dos Reis Católicos XVth *Parador* ❻ Pazo de Raxoi XVIIIth *Presendencia da Xunta* ❼ Colexio de Fonseca XVIth *universidade y claustro* ❽ Capela y Fonte de Santiago ❾ Casa do Deán XVIIIth *Oficina do Peregrino* (*original*). ❿ Casa Canónica *museo Peregrinacións.* ⓫ Mosteiro de San Paio de Antealtares XVth *Museo de Arte Sacra.* ⓬ S.Maria Salomé XIIth.

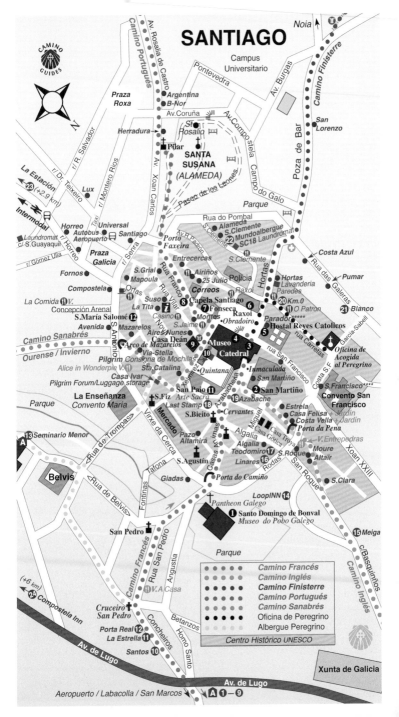

Personal Reflections: "It is solved by walking" *solvitur ambulando*
St.Augustine

PILGRIM ASSOCIATIONS:

UK: The Confraternity of St. James +44 [0]2079 289 988 e-mail: *office@csj.org.uk* website: *www.csj.org.uk* site in English with online bookshop.
IRELAND: The Camino Society Ireland: *www.caminosociety.ie*
U.S.A. American Pilgrims on the Camino. *www.americanpilgrims.org*
CANADA: Canadian Company of Pilgrims Canada. *www.santiago.ca*
SOUTH AFRICA: Confraternity of St. James of SA *www.csjofsa.za.org*
AUSTRALIA: Australian Friends of the Camino *www.afotc.org*

SANTIAGO:

Pilgrim Office *oficinadelperegrino.com/en*
Tourism: *www.santiagoturismo.com*
Luggage storage & transfer / forum & meeting space *www.casaivar.com*
Backpack storage & local tours *www.pilgrim.es* Rúa Nova, 7 (adj. cathedral)

INTERVIEWS WITH JOHN BRIERLEY:

The Camino Cafe Podcast: *www.leighbrennan.com*
Camino Guides: *www.caminoguides.com* under *Your Guide* and *Community*

PILGRIM WEBSITES: (in English) loosely connected with the Way of St. James or with the theme of pilgrimage that you may find helpful.

Camino News: Largest English online camino forum *www.caminodesantiago.me*
The British Pilgrimage Trust: *www.britishpilgrimage.org*
Gatekeeper Trust personal & planetary healing *www.gatekeeper.org.uk*
The Beloved CommUnity *www.belovedcommunity.org* spiritual peacemaking
Findhorn Foundation personal and planetary transformation *www.findhorn.org*
Peace Pilgrim Her life and work *www.peacepilgrim.com*
The Quest A Guide to the Spiritual Journey *www.thequest.org.uk*

ALBERGUE, HOSTAL AND HOTEL BOOKING SITES:

List of albergues open in Winter: *www.aprinca.com/alberguesinvierno/*
Albergues: *www.onlypilgrims.com/en*
Hostals: *www.hostelworld.com*
Paradores: *www.paradore.es*
Hotels: *www.booking.com*
Christian Hospitality Network: *http://en.ephatta.com*

PILGRIM AND BACKPACK TRANSFERS / STORES:

Spanish Postal Service: *http://www.elcaminoconcorreos.com/en/*
Pilbeo: *www.pilbeo.com*
Sarria to Santiago: *www.xacotrans.com*

BIBLIOGRAPHY: Some reading with waymarks to the inner path include:

A Course In Miracles (A.C.I.M.) *Text, Workbook for Students and Manual for Teachers*. Foundation for Inner Peace.

The Art of Pilgrimage *The Seeker's Guide to Making Travel Sacred*, Phil Cousineau. Element Books

Anam Cara *Spiritual wisdom from the Celtic world,* John O'Donohue. Bantam.

A New Earth *Awakening to Your Life's Purpose*, Eckhart Tolle. Penguin Books

A Brief History of Everything *Integrating the partial visions of specialists into a new understanding of the meaning and significance of life*, Ken Wilber.

Care of the Soul *How to add depth and meaning to your everyday life,* Thomas Moore. Piatkus

Conversations with God Neale Donald Walsch. Hodder & Stoughton

From the Holy Mountain *A Journey in the Shadow of Byzantium*, William Dalrymple. Flamingo

Going Home *Jesus and the Buddha as brothers*, Thich Nhat Hanh. Rider Books

Loving What Is *Four Questions That Can Change Your Life*, Byron Katie. Rider

Handbook for the Soul *A collection of wisdom from over 30 celebrated spiritual writers*. Piatkus

The Hero with a Thousand Faces *An examination, through ancient myths, of man's eternal struggle for identity,* Joseph Campbell. Fontana Press

How to Know God *The Soul's Journey into the Mystery of Mysteries*, Deepak Chopra. Rider

Jesus and the Lost Goddess *The Secret Teachings of the Original Christians*, Timothy Freke & Peter Gandy. Three Rivers Press

The Journey Home *The Obstacles to Peace*, Kenneth Wapnick. Foundation for A Course In Miracles

The Mysteries *Rudolf Steiner's writings on Spiritual Initiation*, Andrew Welburn. Floris Books

Mysticism *The Nature and Development of Spiritual Consciousness,* Evelyn Underhill. Oneworld

Building Intuitive Consciousness *The Inner Camino as an Existential Journey*, Sara Hollwey & Jill Brierley. Transpersonal Press.

No Destination *Autobiography (of a pilgrimage)*, Satish Kumar. Green Books

Pilgrimage *Adventures of the Spirit*, Various Authors. Travellers' Tales

Paths of the Christian Mysteries *From Compostela to the New World*, Virginia Sease and Manfred Schmidt-Brabant. Temple Lodge

The Pilgrimage *A Contemporary Quest for Ancient Wisdom*. Paulo Coelho

Peace Pilgrim *Her Life and Work* Friends of Peace Pilgrim. Ocean Tree Books

Pilgrim in Aquarius David Spangler. Findhorn Press

Pilgrim Stories *On and Off the Road to Santiago*. Nancy Louise Frey. University of California Press.

Pilgrim in Time *Mindful Journeys to Encounter the Sacred*. Rosanne Keller.

The Power of Now *A Guide to Spiritual Enlightenment*, Eckhart Tolle. New World

Peace is Every Step *The path of mindfulness in everyday life*, Thich Nhat Hanh.

Phases *The Spiritual Rhythms in Adult Life*, Bernard Lievegoed. Sophia Books

Sacred Contracts *Awakening Your Divine Potential*, Caroline Myss. Bantam

Sacred Roads *Adventures from the Pilgrimage Trail*, Nicholas Shrady. Viking

Secrets of God *Writings of Hildegard of Bingen*. Shambhala

Silence of the Heart *Dialogues with Robert Adams*. Acropolis Books

The Gift of Change *Spiritual Guidance for a Radically New Life*, Marianne Williamson. Element Books

The Prophet. Kahlil Gibran. Mandarin

The Reappearance of the Christ. Alice Bailey. Lucis Press.

The Road Less Travelled *A new Psychology of Love*, M. Scott Peck. Arrow

The Soul's Code *In Search of Character & Calling*, James Hillman. Bantam

Wandering Joy *Meister Eckhart's Mystical Philosophy*. Lindisfarne Press

RETURNING HOME: *Some inner thoughts ...*

It is possible that after a week of walking our outer appearance might have changed, it is also possible that the way we perceive the world has gone through some metamorphosis. This inner transformation may well deepen as the lessons we learnt along the way become more fully integrated. While an obvious purpose of pilgrimage is to bring about an inner shift, it is also possible that our familiar world will no longer support this inner change. This realisation might engender different emotions as we come to see that choices may have to be made that could alter our previous way of life – what we do, where we work, who we live with, our social circuit, where and how we pray or meditate. Indeed the whole purpose, focus and direction of our life may have altered. This may be intimidating to those who previously knew us *the way we were*. Change threatens the status quo but the biggest challenge may be to hold fast to our new understanding garnered from the insights we learnt along the way.

Whatever our individual experiences it is likely that we will be in a heightened state of consciousness and sensitivity. We should resist squeezing our itinerary and the feeling we need to rush back into our usual pattern of work and general lifestyle – this can be a crucial moment. How often do we witness change in ourselves and others only to see fear come and rob us of our new understanding and orientation. Perhaps this is the time to revisit the Self-assessment questionnaire and recall the original purpose and intention of our pilgrimage. If this was, for example, *to come closer to God*, then we should not be surprised if everything that could get in the way of that high invocation is removed from our life, or at least challenged!

Essentially, we are all on a journey of rediscovery of our Essential Nature – our spiritual reality as we begin opening to the knowledge of Higher Worlds. Remember that we have collectively been asleep a long time. While change *can* happen in the twinkling of an eye, it is often experienced as a slow and painful process. The main challenge to our new perspective is likely to be the twin demons of fear and lethargy. The extent to which we hold onto a new way of looking at the world is measured by how far we are prepared to hold onto our truth in the face of opposition – sometimes even from those who profess to love us.

Of course our inner changes may not be so dramatic or those around us may likewise be engaged in inner work and so, far from feeling threatened, may welcome your shift with open arms and hearts – in this case you are blessed indeed. However, it would still be well to remember that these supportive others may not have spent a week walking an ancient spiritual path surrounded by the silence of nature. Take time to integrate back into your life and nurture yourself. Build up a network of fellow pilgrims who can empathise with how you might be feeling and can actively support you. Know that change is nearly always seen as a threat within consensus society. Know also that if you try and change another to your new viewpoint you can aggravate the sense of loss and alienation felt by that other – this is all part of the journey and grist for the mill. Ultimately you can only be responsible for your own actions and re-actions. You cannot be responsible for the experience of others.

This guidebook is dedicated to awakening beyond human consciousness. It was born out of an existential crisis and the perceived need for a time to reflect on the purpose of life and its direction. Collectively devoid of inner-connectedness and a sense of the sacred, we live in a spiritual vacuum of our own making. While ensnared by our outer-directed materialistic world, we unwittingly hold the key to the door of our self-made prison. We can walk free any time we choose. We have been so long separated from our divine origins that we have forgotten what freedom feels like. In our fear of the unknown we choose to limit the potential of each new day to the familiarity of our prison surroundings. Perhaps *El Camino* will reveal the key to your own inner awakening.

As you take a well deserved rest at the end of the long road to the end of the way the question might well arise, 'Is the journey over or just beginning?' Whatever answer you receive will doubtless be right for you at this time. I wish you well in your search for the Truth and your journey Home and extend my humble blessings to a fellow pilgrim on the path and leave you with the words of *J R R Tolkein* from The Lord of the Rings:

> *The Road goes ever on and on*
> *Down from the door where it began.*
> *Now far ahead the Road has gone,*
> *And I must follow, if I can,*
> *Pursuing it with wary feet,*
> *Until it joins some larger way,*
> *Where many paths and errands meet.*
> *And whither then? I cannot say.*

The breeze at dawn has something to tell you. Don't go back to sleep.
                                                                                Rumi

12 Caminos de Santiago

① Camino Francés* **778** km
St. Jean – Santiago
Camino Invierno*
Ponferrada – Santiago **275** km

② Chemin de **Paris 1000** km
Paris – St. Jean via Tours

③ Chemin de **Vézelay 900** km
Vezélay – St. Jean via Bazas

④ Chemin du **Puy 740** km
Le Puy-en-Velay – St. Jean
Ext. to Geneva, Budapest

⑤ Chemin d'**Arles 750** km
Arles – Somport Pass
Camino Aragonés **160** km
Somport Pass – Óbanos
Camí San Jaume **600** km
Port de Selva – Jaca
Camino del Piamonte **515** km
Narbonne - Lourdes - St. Jean

⑥ Camino de **Madrid 320** km
Madrid – Sahagún

Camino de Levante 900 km
Valencia – Zamora
Alt. via Cuenca – Burgos

⑦ Camino **Mozárabe 390** km
Granada – Mérida
(Málaga alt. via Baena)

⑧ Via de la **Plata 1,000** km
Seville – Santiago
Camino Sanabrés Ourense **110** km

⑨ Camino Portugués *Central** **640** km
Lisboa – Porto 389 km
Porto – Santiago 251 km
Camino Portugués *Costa** **320** km
Porto – Santiago
via Caminha & **Variante Espiritual***

⑩ Camino Finisterre* **86** km
Santiago – Finisterre
via – Muxía – Santiago **114** km

⑪ Camino Inglés* **120** km
Ferrol & Coruna – Santiago

⑫ Camino del **Norte 830** km
Irún – Santiago via Gijón

Camino Primitivo 320 km
Oviedo – Lugo – Melide